*American*

Frederic Martin's book comes at a crucial time in history when the Evangelical Church is waking up and realizing the huge negative impact of Christian Zionism on the Church, on America, and on politics in the Middle East. It is my hope that Martin's clear, easy-to-read style and his fairness in presenting the argument will cause many of us Evangelicals to search our hearts and lead us to repent for all the pain, wars, and injuries our theology and eschatology have inflicted on millions of people in the Middle East and in North Africa.

REV. ALEX AWAD
DEAN OF STUDENTS, BETHLEHEM BIBLE COLLEGE
PASTOR, EAST JERUSALEM BAPTIST CHURCH

Dr. Fred Martin's blend of pastoral experience, along with keen academic abilities, makes him eminently suited to write this book. A majority of Christians today would still give the present nation of Israel their unqualified and unquestioned support, politically and otherwise. Martin's book is a desperately needed and sane call to reexamine those assumptions from a sound biblical, theological, and pastoral perspective. Hopefully this book will receive a wide reading.

DR. DAVID MATHEWSON
ASSOCIATE PROFESSOR OF NEW TESTAMENT, DENVER SEMINARY

This book brings joy to me—and heartache. The joy: this is a thoughtful, scholarly, and biblical analysis of issues swirling within the evangelical community regarding prophecy as well as politics. It is readable and succinct, a welcomed resource for the concerned person. Then the heartache: Among many evangelicals, there is a brittleness, even harshness, when it comes to responding to the Israeli-Palestinian situation. The concern to "defend" the biblical narrative has, too often, resulted in a misappropriation of that narrative. Will we be willing to look anew at the Scriptures and humbly allow them to speak to us—trustworthy as they are, without our preconceived "stances"?

DR. THOMAS J. BOWER,
PAST PRESIDENT OF OAK HILLS CHRISTIAN COLLEGE

# American Evangelicals
& Modern Israel

# American Evangelicals & Modern Israel

*A Plea for Tough Love*

Frederic M. Martin

Deep River
B O O K S

American Evangelicals and Modern Israel
Copyright © 2016 Frederic M. Martin

All rights reserved. No part of this book may be reproduced in any form without permission in writing from the publisher, except in the case of brief quotations embodied in critical articles or reviews.

Published by
Deep River Books
Sisters, Oregon
www.deepriverbooks.com

Unless otherwise indicated, Scripture references are from The Holy Bible®, New International Version®, NIV. Copyright © 1973, 1978, 1984, 2011 by Biblica, Inc.™ Used by permission. All rights reserved worldwide.

Scripture quotations marked NASB are from the NEW AMERICAN STANDARD BIBLE®. Copyright © 1960, 1962, 1963, 1968, 1971, 1972, 1973, 1975, 1977, 1995 by The Lockman Foundation. Used by permission.

Scripture quotations marked ESV are from *The Holy Bible*, English Standard Version, copyright © 2001 by Crossway Bibles, a division of Good News Publishers. Used by permission. All rights reserved.

ISBN: 9781940269757
Library of Congress: 2015959621

Printed in USA
Cover design by Joe Bailen

*To Berta,*
loving and faithful
wife, companion, and friend

# Acknowledgments

I must express my indebtedness to those who helped me bring this book to completion.

My thanks go to those who first read the manuscript and critiqued it: Laura Engelstad, Christy Oelslager, Wayne Potter, Karl Salscheider, and Barb Smith. Tom Bower, Jim McRae and Jacob Thomas also offered wise suggestions on how to improve it.

Others encouraged me simply by expressing their interest in my research: Steve and Evelyn Biles, Josie Fultz, Anna and Doug Johnson, Becky Kangas, Andy Kellogg, Jerry Johnson, and Jerry Loud. Rachel Starr Thomson, my editor at Deep River Books, offered many valuable suggestions on how to improve the content and clarity of this book. I also want to acknowledge the encouragement I received from my four children and their spouses. Special thanks go to my daughter Katie for creating the book's maps.

I would be remiss if I did not express my gratitude to the members of the Evangelical Free Church of Bemidji, Minnesota. They did not always agree with my conclusions, but they kindly listened to me nonetheless.

All of the people mentioned above have in some way contributed to this book, but I do bear sole responsibility for the final product.

Finally and above all, I thank my wife, Berta, who supported and encouraged me in this project and was never afraid to ask, "And how do you know you are right?"

# Contents

Introduction: The Whole Story? . . . . . . . . . . . . . . . . . . . . . . . . . . . 13

## Part One
## Past and Present

Chapter 1: The Israeli Narrative . . . . . . . . . . . . . . . . . . . . . . . . . . . 17
Chapter 2: The Palestinian Narrative . . . . . . . . . . . . . . . . . . . . . . . 33
Chapter 3: The Present Situation . . . . . . . . . . . . . . . . . . . . . . . . . . 49

## Part Two
## Bible and Theology

Chapter 4: The Old Testament and Modern Israel . . . . . . . . . . . . . 77
Chapter 5: The Old Testament Fulfilled . . . . . . . . . . . . . . . . . . . . . 87
Chapter 6: The Promise to Abraham Fulfilled . . . . . . . . . . . . . . . . 101
Chapter 7: What about Bible Prophecy? . . . . . . . . . . . . . . . . . . . . 117
Chapter 8: Is This Replacement Theology? . . . . . . . . . . . . . . . . . . 139

## Part Three
## Evangelicals and Injustice

Chapter 9: A Plea for Tough Love . . . . . . . . . . . . . . . . . . . . . . . . . 155
Glossary . . . . . . . . . . . . . . . . . . . . . . . . . . . . . . . . . . . . . . . . . . . . 175
Endnotes . . . . . . . . . . . . . . . . . . . . . . . . . . . . . . . . . . . . . . . . . . . 179

*Introduction*
# The Whole Story?

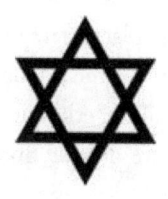

On a sunny day in May of 1985, I was eating a box lunch in a rest area overlooking the Sharon Plain and the Mediterranean Sea. I had gone to Israel to take a three-week course on historical geography, and that day our class was on a field trip in the hills west of Jerusalem. While we ate lunch, one person mentioned what a scenic spot it was. Our teacher made a brief comment in response. She told us that prior to 1948 and the founding of the modern nation of Israel, that rest area had been the site of an Arab village.

It was just a brief comment. She didn't elaborate on it, but it stuck with me.

On one hand, I understood why the Israelis had torn the village down. It was a strategic site. An army positioned there could effectively control all the traffic on the road below that led from the Mediterranean Sea up to Jerusalem.

But that simple comment also made me start thinking about modern Israel in ways I had never thought of it before. The Israelis had destroyed at least one Arab village and displaced all of its residents. Were there other Arab villages that had also been demolished? I have learned since then that hundreds of Palestinian villages were destroyed and thousands of their residents left homeless. This didn't just happen to Muslims. I've read the stories of Palestinian Christians who were treated the same way.

Prior to the teacher's comment I had read that in the 1948 war the Israelis encouraged the Arabs to remain in their villages. It was the Arab leaders who urged them to flee. If they had only listened to the Israelis instead, 700,000 Arab villagers would never have been displaced from their homes. Now I started to wonder if that was true.

Over the past thirty years I've taken additional trips to Israel, and I have read books written by both Palestinians and Israelis. I have often wondered why Americans seem unaware of the whole story of what happened in the Middle East during the twentieth century. And why are Americans so misinformed about what is taking place there now?

Even more troubling to me is the unqualified support that well-intentioned evangelical Christians in America give to the policies of the modern nation of Israel. Bible verses are quickly quoted, and appeals are made to unfulfilled Bible prophecies. Those who question modern Israel are suspected of being anti-Semitic. But the quotes and appeals are decidedly one-sided, and the accusations are leveled without explanation or qualification. Again I wonder: Why aren't evangelical Christians taking into consideration all that the Bible says on the subject?

I've written this book for other believers in Jesus Christ. Part 1 begins with two opposing narratives of the relevant events of the twentieth century. The Israeli perspective which most Americans are familiar with is followed by the Palestinian point of view, which is rarely heard in the United States. The section concludes with an analysis of what is happening now in Israel, the West Bank, and Gaza.

Part 2 delves into the theological and ethical dimensions of the controversy. What does the Old Testament teach about Israel? How has the coming of Christ changed or modified the application of that Old Testament teaching? What relevance should Bible prophecy have for believers' understanding of the contemporary Middle East? What is Replacement Theology, and is it inevitably anti-Semitic?

In the final part, the United States' unqualified support for Israel is examined and critiqued. Many Christians are surprised to learn that prominent individuals within both the Israeli and American Jewish communities are critical of the way that Israel treats Palestinians. American evangelicals should add their voices to the protest. In obedience to God they should reexamine their unconditional support for Israel and urge the United States to practice tough love that is pro-Israel and pro-Palestine—pro-peace and pro-justice.

# Part One
# Past and Present

*Chapter One*
# The Israeli Narrative

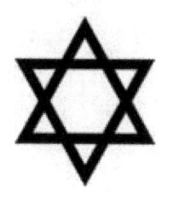

*"For this is what the Lord Almighty says [about Israel]:
'...whoever touches you touches the apple of his eye.'"*

ZECHARIAH 2:8

ONE DAY IN THE MID-1960S I was looking for something to read. For no particular reason I picked a novel off my parents' bookshelf. It was Leon Uris's bestseller, *Exodus*. Written in 1958, it told the story of the founding of the modern nation of Israel. I found myself captivated by the novel and also by Israel itself. How astounding that a nation had come back into existence after an absence of two thousand years! What insurmountable odds had been courageously overcome in order to establish Israel in its ancient homeland! The founding of the nation was breathtaking and inspiring.

A few years later a family friend invited me to attend an intensive two-week Bible class. I attended with some reluctance, but much to my own amazement I came to faith in Jesus Christ through that class. I was suddenly excited about God and filled with a desire to live with him and for him. I got up early in the morning to read the Bible. I eagerly attended Bible studies with friends. I devoured all the books I could get my hands on that would teach me more about my Lord and his work in this world.

I read with fascination *The Late Great Planet Earth* by Hal Lindsey. Lindsey explained the Old Testament's predictions about the Middle East and showed how they were coming true. God's prophets in the Old Testament had predicted the restoration of the Jews to their homeland. The establishment of

Israel in 1948 was a miraculous fulfillment of those ancient prophecies. The capture of Jerusalem in 1967 was another sign from God that the end times were coming soon. "Keep your eyes on the Middle East,"[1] Lindsey advised. I took his advice to heart. God was obviously at work in modern Israel!

As they did for many others at that time, *Exodus* and *The Late Great Planet Earth* convinced me to become a staunch supporter of Israel.[2] God had declared through his prophet Zechariah that Israel was "the apple of his eye." The Bible taught it, and the story of Israel's founding in 1948 confirmed it. To love Israel was to obey God's will.

## The Eyeglasses of History

To many people history is nothing but the boring recitation of irrelevant facts about the past, but it should not be so quickly dismissed. History can be compared to a set of eyeglasses through which people view current events. What we think has taken place in the past shapes the way we view what is happening in the present. It also prepares us for what we think will happen in the future. That is particularly true when it comes to the Israeli-Palestinian conflict.

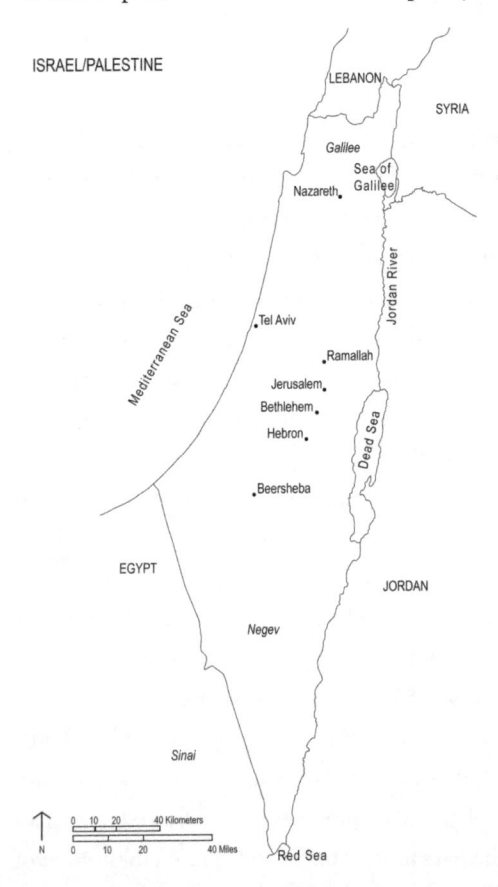

In order to understand the situation in Palestine and Israel today, the events of the nineteenth and twentieth centuries have to be taken into consideration. The current conflict did not arise in a vacuum. Both Israelis and Palestinians have their own version of those historical events. This chapter and the one that follows present both narratives, *with each deliberately set out in as strong and convincing a manner as possible*. Both narratives need to be heard and *felt* in order to understand the very different perspectives that inform and shape the Israeli and Palestinian attitude toward the conflict today.[3]

We will begin, as the title of this chapter indicates, with the Israeli narrative.

## THE RISE OF ZIONISM

In the late nineteenth century, Jews started to move back to their ancient homeland due to persecution in eastern Europe and Russia. Approximately 24,000 Jews lived in Palestine in 1882.[4] Over the next sixty years there were five waves of *aliyah* (Hebrew for "going up"; used to describe the Jewish "return to Zion").

| Date | Number of Immigrants | Nations of Origin |
| --- | --- | --- |
| 1st Aliyah 1882 – 1903 | 25,000 | Russia, Romania, Kurdistan, and Yemen |
| 2nd Aliyah 1904 – 1914 | 40,000 | Russia and Poland |
| 3rd Aliyah 1919 – 1923 | 35,000 | 53% Russia<br>36% Poland<br>11% Lithuania, Romania, and Western and Central Europe |
| 4th Aliyah 1924 – 1928 | 67,000 | Poland |
| 5th Aliyah 1929 – 1939 | 250,000 | Germany, Austria, and other countries |

[5]

Even though some rabbis and writers had earlier advocated the establishment of a Jewish state in Palestine, the beginning of the Zionist movement is usually dated to 1896 with the publication of Theodore Herzl's book *The Jewish State*. Herzl was a journalist in Austria who was sent to Paris to cover the military trial of the French military officer Alfred Dreyfus. Dreyfus, a Jew, had been accused of treason and found guilty by the French courts. Herzl and others were convinced that the conviction was not warranted by the evidence but resulted from the ingrained anti-Semitism that characterized European civilization. Herzl thought that such deep-seated hatred could never be overcome. Therefore, he concluded that the only hope for freedom from discrimination was the establishment of a Jewish nation.

Herzl was more than a writer; he was an activist. On August 29, 1897, he convened the First Zionist Congress in Basel, Switzerland. Over two hundred delegates from twenty-four countries attended. A Jewish nation was now more than a dream; it had become a movement. Herzl claimed to have accomplished even more. He wrote in his diary, "At Basel I founded the Jewish State."[6]

In his book Herzl had suggested Palestine or Argentina as possible locations for the Jewish homeland.[7] He was willing to consider any territory that offered a haven from anti-Semitism. In August 1903 England offered part of Uganda to the Zionists. That offer was seriously considered and led to a division within the young Zionist movement. It was eventually rejected. Only the biblical land of Palestine would be acceptable as the Jewish homeland.[8]

Zionist Congresses continued to be held in subsequent years, and Herzl asked for support from international leaders: the German kaiser, the Ottoman sultan, the Italian king, and the Catholic pope. The warmest response to Herzl's proposal came from evangelical Christians in England. Even in the early years of the Reformation, Protestants had looked forward to the eventual turning of the Jews to Jesus the Messiah.[9] Some teachers also predicted their physical restoration to the land. For example, in 1828 Henry Drummond published *Dialogues on Prophecy*, in which he predicted that God was about to judge the church and that "during the time that these judgements are falling upon Christendom, the Jews will be restored to the land."[10]

Theodore Herzl died in 1904, but the movement he had begun continued to grow. It achieved a major breakthrough during World War I. On November 2, 1917, Arthur Balfour, the British foreign secretary, wrote an official letter that included a statement that has become known as the Balfour Declaration:

> His Majesty's Government view with favour the establishment in Palestine of a national home for the Jewish people, and will use their best endeavours to facilitate the achievement of this object, it being clearly understood that nothing shall be done which may

prejudice the civil and religious rights of existing non-Jewish communities in Palestine, or the rights and political status enjoyed by Jews in any other country.[11]

The Balfour Declaration was the first official statement by any European government that gave support to the establishment of a Jewish national home. Just five weeks later, on December 11, 1917, the British army under General Allenby captured the city of Jerusalem. With the crumbling of the Ottoman Empire in World War I, a Jewish nation now seemed to be a real possibility.

In February of 1919, the Paris Peace Conference granted Great Britain authority over Palestine. The conference also endorsed the establishment of a Jewish homeland as expressed in the Balfour Declaration. The following year, the Allies met in San Remo, Italy, to discuss the future of the territories that had been under Ottoman control. They endorsed the Balfour Declaration and the British Mandate. In 1922 the League of Nations confirmed those decisions. The Ottoman Empire had ceased to exist, and Great Britain was internationally recognized as the legal authority over Palestine.[12]

The Zionists desired a homeland where they would be safe from the discrimination and persecution they had experienced in Europe and Russia, but those who immigrated to Palestine did not find peace in their new homeland. Even though Arabs vastly outnumbered Jews, they felt threatened by Jewish immigration.

| Year | Arab Population | Jewish Population |
| --- | --- | --- |
| 1918 | 688,000 | 60,000 |
| 1922 | 760,000 | 84,000 |
| 1931 | 868,000 | 175,000 |
| 1939 | 1,070,000 | 460,000 |

[13]

In 1920–1921 the Arabs attacked Jewish settlements in Galilee and rioted in Jerusalem. Additional Arab riots occurred in 1929 in the cities of Jerusalem, Hebron, and Safed. In April of 1936 Arab riots broke out against the British. The revolt continued until May 1939. According to Israeli historian Benny Morris, "It was to be the biggest and most protracted uprising against the British in any country in the Middle East, and the most significant in Palestinian history until the anti-Israel Intifada fifty years later."[14]

Faced with the problem of governing a land where tensions ran so high, the British looked for some kind of resolution. In November of 1936 they formed the Peel Commission to determine the cause of the "disturbances" in Palestine and to propose a solution. Jewish representatives assured the commission that they wanted to create a Jewish national home without causing undue suffering for the Arabs, but the Arabs boycotted most of the commission meetings.[15] The Peel Commission published its report in July 1937 and announced that no solution to the conflict was possible. Therefore, it recommended that the land be partitioned between the Jews and the Arabs. Under the leadership of David Ben-Gurion, the Jews said that they were willing to accept the plan, but the Arabs strongly opposed it. By the summer of 1938 the recommendations of the Peel Commission had hit a dead end.

Great Britain tried again in late 1938 by publishing a government White Paper that rejected partition into two nations. In its place, the British recommended the establishment of an Arab state in the Samarian and Judean highlands and the creation of a Jewish state along a thin stretch of the Mediterranean coast. The British would continue to rule Galilee, Jerusalem, Bethlehem, Jaffa, and the southern desert region. New limits would be placed on Jewish immigration.

Now it was the Zionist leaders who objected. They argued that the British had retreated from the Balfour Declaration and the mandate given to it by the League of Nations. Great Britain had reneged on the idea of a sufficiently spacious national home for the Jews. Arab violence had intimidated the British at the same time that Jews in Europe were continuing to suffer from anti-Semitism.[16]

While the British flip-flopped in the Middle East, Hitler and the Nazis embarked on their goal of exterminating the Jews in Europe. Starting in 1939 and continuing for the next six years, the Nazis hunted down Jews, shipped them to concentration camps, and ruthlessly slaughtered them. Six million Jews—more than one third of the Jewish people worldwide—perished while the world did little if anything to rescue them. Never had the necessity for a Jewish homeland been more obvious.

By 1947 the British were tired of trying to govern Palestine. In February they announced that they would turn the problem over to the United Nations. That international body formed the United Nations Special Committee on Palestine (UNSCOP). While the committee pursued its own investigation into the situation, tensions continued to build between Jews and British soldiers in the land. One event in particular influenced UNSCOP's thinking and seemed to symbolize nineteenth- and twentieth-century Jewish history. The *Exodus*, a Jewish ship packed with 4,500 survivors of the Holocaust, was not only refused permission by the British to land in Palestine but was actually compelled to return to Germany.[17]

The UNSCOP majority report recommended that Palestine be partitioned into Jewish and Arab states with an international zone declared for the Holy Places in Jerusalem and Bethlehem. The British government announced that it would not take responsibility for enforcing such a partition and that it planned to remove all its troops from Palestine by May 15, 1948.[18]

## The Birth of the Nation

On November 29, 1947, the United Nations passed Resolution 181, which partitioned the land of Palestine into two states. On May 14, 1948, David Ben-Gurion declared Israel to be a free and independent nation. In spite of opposition from his advisors in the State Department, President Harry Truman immediately declared the United

States' recognition of the new nation. He was the first world leader to do so. The Jewish homeland had become a reality.

Israel was immediately plunged into war. The Arabs refused to accept the United Nations' partition plan, and five Arab countries attacked the fledgling nation. The 640,000 Jews in Israel were surrounded by Arab nations with populations totaling over 80 million.[19] Yet over the course of the next few months, Israel proved victorious. In the course of just fifty years a homeland for the Jews had grown from a dream to a movement to an established nation.

With the founding of the nation came a problem that has plagued Israel ever since: Palestinian refugees. Approximately 700,000 Palestinians lost their homes in the war and became residents of refugee camps in the nations surrounding Israel. Was Israel to blame? One evangelical supporter of modern Israel, Marvin Rosenthal, summarizes Israel's innocence:

> In the months preceding Israel's May of 1948 declaration of nationhood, many Palestinian Arabs chose, of their own volition, to abandon their homes and lands in what was eventually to become the State of Israel. Under the United Nations partition plan, they had the right of full citizenship in the new emerging State of Israel. However under the influence of surrounding Arab nations, they were urged to leave their homes and travel the short distance to the West Bank or the Gaza Strip…
>
> Those who chose to remain in Israel (or their families) are there to this day, enjoying the benefits of citizenship and a standard of living far higher than that of surrounding Arab nations.[20]

The Arab nations bordering Israel could have accepted the refugees into their countries just as Israel welcomed Jewish refugees from Europe, the Middle East, and Africa, but they refused to do so. Instead, they chose to prolong the refugees' misery.[21]

## The Conflict Continues

Israel had been established, but peace was yet to be found. In the following decades additional wars would be fought because of the neighboring nations' unrelenting opposition to Israel's existence.

In 1956 the Egyptian dictator Gamal Abdel Nasser stopped Israeli vessels from entering or exiting the Gulf of Aqaba and seized the British-owned Suez Canal. Israel joined Britain and France in a military operation that removed this threat to Israel's safety.[22]

In 1964 the Palestine Liberation Organization (PLO) was created. Its founding charter states its unyielding opposition to Israel:

ARTICLE 17: The partitioning of Palestine, which took place in 1947, and the establishment of Israel are illegal and null and void, regardless of the loss of time, because they were contrary to the will of the Palestinian people and its natural right to its homeland, and were in violation of the basic principles embodied in the Charter of the United Nations, foremost among which is the right to self-determination.

ARTICLE 18: The Balfour Declaration, the Palestine Mandate System, and all that has been based on them are considered null and void…

ARTICLE 19: Zionism is a colonialist movement in its inception, aggressive and expansionist in its goal, racist in its configurations, and fascist in its means and aims. Israel, in its capacity as the spearhead of this destructive movement and as the pillar of colonialism, is a permanent source of tension and turmoil in the Middle East.[23]

June of 1967 found Israel threatened by Egypt as well as Jordan and Syria. Egypt's Nasser had once again closed the Straits of Tiran to Israeli ships and issued threats to the peace and security of Israel. The Israeli Defense Force decided to launch a preemptive attack. In the course of six dramatic days Israel overwhelmed its enemies and took control of the Sinai Peninsula, Gaza, the Golan Heights, the West Bank, and East Jerusalem. Israel emerged from the war as the most powerful military power in the Middle East.[24]

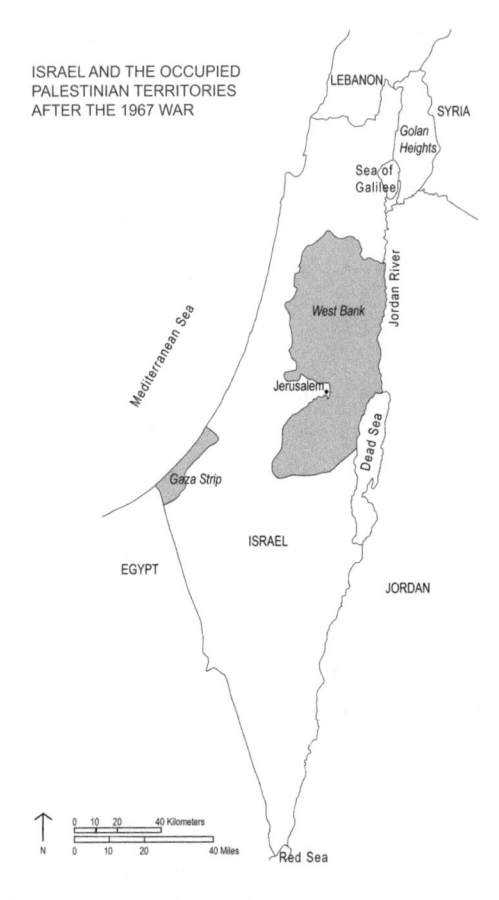

While the 1967 Six Day War was a stunning military victory, it created a new problem for Israel. What was the nation going to do with all of the Arabs who lived in the territories it had won on the battlefield? One Israeli writer summarizes what Israel faced:

> Following the 1967 war Israel was in control of large territories populated by Arabs. East Jerusalem and 28 Arab villages on the West Bank were annexed to the state, and the newly occupied territories included the West Bank…and the Gaza Strip…. In a census taken in 1967 nearly a million Arabs lived in these territories—595,000 in the West Bank and 389,700 in Gaza.[25]

After the Six Day War, Israel was prepared to give up large areas of occupied territories in order to have peace. No definite offers were made regarding the West Bank and Gaza Strip, but Israel expressed a willingness to deal with those territories at a later time. The Arab nations demonstrated no interest in compromise. They met in the Sudanese city of Khartoum in August and September of 1967 and issued what became known as the Three Nos: no peace with Israel, no recognition of Israel, and no negotiations with Israel.[26]

Opposition to Israel continued unabated. The PLO established its own terrorist group, Black September. The world watched in horror as it held hostage and then murdered eleven members of the Israeli Olympic team at the 1972 Munich Olympics. In the following year Egypt and Syria launched a surprise attack on Israel on the holiest day of the year. At first it appeared that the Yom Kippur War of 1973 would end in a humiliating defeat for the Jewish nation, but the Israel Defense Force responded courageously and emerged victorious.

## Negotiations for Peace

A hopeful step toward peace in the Middle East took place on November 9, 1977. Egyptian leader Anwar Sadat announced to his nation's parliament that he was prepared "to go to the end of the earth" and "to the Knesset itself" in search of peace. Menachem Begin, prime minister of Israel, invited Sadat to Israel, and the invitation was accepted. On November 19 Sadat flew to Israel. He addressed the Knesset, Israel's parliament, on the following day and urged Israel to work with him in establishing peace between their countries. This bold initiative eventually led to Sadat and Begin meeting with President Jimmy Carter at the White House on March 26, 1979, in order to sign a peace treaty between Egypt and Israel.[27]

A major step toward peace had taken place, but Israel remained on alert—Egypt had been far from the only threat. From 1982 to 1985 Israel found itself at war in Lebanon. At this time the PLO had its headquarters in Beirut. After repeated rocket attacks, Israel invaded Lebanon in order to establish a twenty-five-mile-wide security zone along the Israeli-Lebanese border. In 1985 it withdrew to a security zone just four miles wide.

In August of 1988 the terrorist organization known as Hamas published its covenant. It rejected the PLO as the sole representative of the Palestinian people, and it refused to consider any compromise with the nation of Israel. Hamas called for a holy war to destroy Israel.[28]

In spite of the Palestinian protests and the uprising known as the Intifada (Arabic for "shaking off"), which started in 1987, secret talks between Israel and the PLO took place in Oslo early in 1993. These talks led to the signing of the Declaration of Principles or Oslo Accords by PLO Chairman Yasser Arafat and Israeli Prime Minister Yitzhak Rabin at the White House on September 13, 1993. Arafat finally accepted UN Security

Council Resolution 242, which had been passed in 1967 and called for the "termination of all claims or states of belligerency and respect for and acknowledgement of the sovereignty, territorial integrity and political independence of every State in the area and their right to live in peace within secure and recognized boundaries free from threats or acts of violence."[29] In return for Arafat's recognition of Israel's legitimacy and his renunciation of terrorism, Rabin agreed to a plan for peace that would lead to the eventual establishment of a Palestinian state, negotiations over the status of Jerusalem, and resolution of the refugee problem. In 1994 the Nobel Peace Prize was awarded to Arafat, Rabin, and Israel's Foreign Minister, Shimon Peres, for this historical accomplishment. Hope for genuine and permanent peace blossomed.[30]

That hope soon encountered serious roadblocks. Prime Minister Rabin was assassinated by a Jewish extremist on November 4, 1995, and factions among the Palestinians rejected the Oslo Accords. Suicide bombings by Palestinians created grave doubts about the possibility of peace. Negotiations continued but eventually become deadlocked in July of 2000 when Arafat turned down the offer made by Prime Minister Ehud Barak to divide Jerusalem so that it could become the legal capital of Palestine as well as Israel.[31]

## THE CONFLICT RESUMES

The situation continued to deteriorate with the start of the Second Intifada in September 2000. Suicide bombings and other terrorist attacks increased in frequency. Israel responded with Operation Defensive Shield. On March 28, 2002, Israeli forces moved into the West Bank and Gaza to destroy the terrorist network that Arafat had allowed to flourish.[32] In 2002 Israel found it necessary to build its 440-mile-long Separation Barrier to prevent West Bank suicide bombers from terrorizing innocent Israeli citizens. The number of suicide bombings was drastically reduced as a result.

In September of 2005 Prime Minister Ariel Sharon decided that Israel would unilaterally withdraw from Gaza. The Israeli settlements there were dismantled, and Gaza was allowed to govern itself.[33] In 2006, however, the people of Gaza elected a new parliament in which the majority of members were from Hamas, a terrorist organization. In spite of the freedom they were granted, Hamas continues to terrorize Israeli citizens by launching rockets into the city of Sderot.

## Palestinian Life Improves

The Palestinians and their defenders typically portray life in the West Bank and Gaza since 1967 as one of oppression and poverty. Efraim Karsh, a professor at King's College London, cites statistics that demonstrate otherwise:

> ...the number of Palestinians working in Israel rose from zero in 1967 to 66,000 in 1975 and 109,000 by 1986, accounting for 35 percent of the employed population of the West Bank and 45 percent in Gaza. Close to 2,000 industrial plants, employing almost half of the work force, were established in the territories under Israeli rule.
>
> During the 1970's, the West Bank and Gaza constituted the fourth fastest-growing economy in the world... By 1999, Palestinian per-capita income was nearly double Syria's, more than four times Yemen's, and 10 percent higher than Jordan's (one of the better off Arab states). Only the oil-rich Gulf states and Lebanon were more affluent.
>
> Under Israeli rule, the Palestinians also made vast progress in social welfare. Perhaps most significantly, mortality rates in the West Bank and Gaza fell by more than two-thirds between 1970 and 1990, while life expectancy rose from 48 years in 1967 to 72 in 2000... Israeli medical programs reduced the infant-mortality rate of 60 per 1,000 live births in 1968 to 15 per 1,000 in 2000.... And under a systematic program of inoculation, childhood diseases like polio, whooping cough, tetanus, and measles were eradicated.
>
> No less remarkable were advances in the Palestinians' standard of living. By 1986, 92.8 percent of the population in the West Bank and Gaza had electricity around the clock, as compared to 20.5 percent in 1967; 85 percent had running water in dwellings, as compared to 16 percent in 1967; 83.5 percent had electric or gas ranges for cooking, as compared to 4 percent in 1967; and so on for refrigerators, televisions, and cars.

Finally, and perhaps most strikingly, during the two decades preceding the intifada of the late 1980's, the number of schoolchildren in the territories grew by 102 percent, and the number of classes by 99 percent, though the population itself had grown by only 28 percent. Even more dramatic was the progress in higher education. At the time of the Israeli occupation of Gaza and the West Bank, not a single university existed in these territories. By the early 1990's, there were seven such institutions, boasting some 16,500 students.[34]

## The Role of Religion

An ongoing factor in the conflict is the religious one. Three major religions view Jerusalem as their holy city. The Israelis worship at the Western Wall in the Old City, and a few hundred yards away stands the Dome of the Rock. According to Muslims, that site marks the spot where the prophet Muhammad ascended on his Night Journey. The city is also holy to Christians because the Church of the Holy Sepulchre marks the traditional location of Jesus's crucifixion.

Islam plays a crucial role in the Arabs' opposition to Israel's existence.[35] The most prominent example of the Muslims' rejection of Israel comes from Iran, the home of Shi'ite Muslims. The former president of the nation, Mahmoud Ahmadinejad, repeatedly denied that the Nazi Holocaust took place and regularly called for the "elimination of the Zionist regime."[36]

## Israel's Unending Desire

The nation of Israel has longed for peace from the day of its establishment in 1948. In a speech to the United States Congress on May 23, 2011, Prime Minister Benjamin Netanyahu precisely summarized the problem:

> Peace would herald a new day for both our peoples, and it could also make the dream of a broader Arab-Israeli peace a realistic possibility. So now, here's the question. You've got to ask it: If the benefits of peace with the Palestinians are so clear, why has peace eluded us? Because all six Israeli prime ministers since the signing of the Oslo Accords agreed to establish a Palestinian state, myself

included; so why has peace not been achieved?

Because so far, the Palestinians have been unwilling to accept a Palestinian state if it meant accepting a Jewish state alongside it.

You see, our conflict has never been about the establishment of a Palestinian state; it's always been about the existence of the Jewish state. This is what this conflict is about.

In 1947, the U.N. voted to partition the land into a Jewish state and an Arab state. The Jews said yes; the Palestinians said no.

In recent years, the Palestinians twice refused generous offers by Israeli prime ministers to establish a Palestinian state on virtually all the territory won by Israel in the Six Day War. They were simply unwilling to end the conflict.[37]

## Chapter Two
# The Palestinian Narrative

*In a lawsuit the first to speak seems right,
until someone comes forward and cross-examines.*

Proverbs 18:17

One Sunday evening over a hundred people came to church to hear a presentation about Palestine and Israel. I began the evening by asking how many of them had ever heard of the Holocaust. Hands shot up all over the room. I then asked them how many Jews had been killed by the Nazis during World War II. The response was immediate: "Six million." Then I asked the people how many of them had ever heard of the Nakba. A few hesitant hands were raised. I followed that up by asking how many Palestinian lives had been radically altered by it. No one offered an answer.

That simple exercise strengthened my hunch that evangelical Christians in America know the Israeli perspective on twentieth-century events in the Middle East but know little if anything about the Palestinian understanding of that same period of time. In fact, many Christians are not even aware that there is a Palestinian narrative. The Israeli account summarized in the last chapter is all they have ever heard. And it is so convincing! What more needs to be said?

Proverbs 18:17 offers a needed warning: "In a lawsuit the first to speak seems right, until someone comes forward and cross-examines." The Israeli narrative is powerful and moving, but it is not the whole story. We need to allow the Palestinians to "come forward and cross-examine."[38] It too is powerful and convincing.

## Early Jewish Settlers

Lord Shaftesbury, a Christian leader in nineteenth-century England, believed in the restoration of the Jews to their homeland for both political and religious reasons. He was convinced that the conversion of the Jews to Christianity would usher in a worldwide movement toward faith in Jesus Christ. To achieve that goal, Shaftesbury urged British politicians to support Jewish migration to Palestine. Shaftesbury is credited with inspiring the slogan: "A land without a people for a people without a land."[39]

Many Europeans like Shaftesbury believed that Palestine was a barren land that could easily absorb new settlers. No harm would be done to the few residents of the land if Jews migrated to their ancient homeland. In 1891, however, the Jewish writer Ahad Ha'am visited Palestine and wrote, "We abroad are used to believing that Eretz Yisrael [the land of Israel] is now almost totally desolate, a desert that is not sowed.... But in truth that is not the case. Throughout the country it is difficult to find fields that are not sowed."[40] In 1905 Yitzhak Epstein, a Palestinian Jew, delivered a lecture on the "Arab question" at a meeting in Switzerland. He said, "We have forgotten one small matter: There is in our beloved land an entire nation, which has occupied it for hundreds of years and has never thought to leave it."[41] An apocryphal but frequently told story memorably summarizes the problem. Some rabbis sent a deputation to Palestine to survey the land. "The bride is beautiful," they wrote back, "but she is married to another man."[42]

Zionist leaders recognized this problem from the beginning of the movement even though they did not emphasize it. When it was addressed, the solution that was quietly proposed was "transfer," or involuntary exile of the Arabs. Theodore Herzl himself made that suggestion, and Zionist leaders, including David Ben-Gurion, the first prime minister of Israel, endorsed the idea over the next fifty years. Shlomo Ben-Ami, former Israeli foreign minister, observes, "The idea of transfer for the Arabs had a long pedigree in Zionist thought. Moral scruples hardly intervened in what was normally seen as a realistic and logical solution, a matter of expediency."[43]

| Date | Zionist Leader | Statement on "Transfer" |
|---|---|---|
| June 12, 1895 | Theodor Herzl | "We shall endeavor to expel the poor population across the border unnoticed, procuring employment for it in the transit countries, but denying it any employment in our country.... The process of expropriation and the removal of the poor must be carried out discreetly and circumspectly." |
| 1920 | Israel Zangwill | "We cannot allow the Arabs to block so valuable a piece of historic reconstruction.... And therefore we must gently persuade them to 'trek'.... There is no particular reason for the Arabs to cling to these few kilometers. 'To fold their tents' and 'steal away' is their proverbial habit: let them exemplify it now." |
| 1930 | Menachem Usshiskin | "If there are other inhabitants there, they must be transferred to some other place. We must take over the land." |
| June 1938 | David Ben-Gurion | "I support compulsory transfer. I do not see anything immoral in it." |
| 1941 | David Ben-Gurion | "It is impossible to imagine general evacuation [of the Arab population] without compulsion, and brutal compulsion." |
| 1944 | David Ben-Gurion | "Were I asked what should be our program, it would not occur to me to tell them to transfer...because speaking about the matter might harm us...in world opinion, because it might give the impression that there is no room in the Land of Israel without ousting the Arabs and...it would alert and antagonize the Arabs..." |

44 45 46 47 48 49

## THE BALFOUR DECLARATION

The 1917 Balfour Declaration was Britain's promise to the Zionists that they would work toward "the establishment in Palestine of a national home for the Jewish people." It added one important qualification: "it being clearly understood that nothing shall be done which may prejudice the civil and religious rights of existing non-Jewish communities in Palestine."

When taken alone, the Balfour Declaration may sound just, but taken in its historical context three problems emerge.

First, just two years after issuing the famous Declaration, Balfour expanded on his true intentions and indicated his bias toward the Zionists: "Zionism, be it right or wrong, good or bad, is rooted in age-old traditions, in present needs, in future hopes, of far profounder import than the desires and prejudices of the 700,000 Arabs who now inhabit that ancient land."[50]

A second problem with the Balfour Declaration stemmed from the promises Britain had made over a year before to Arab leaders in order to gain their support in fighting the Turks. On August 30, 1915, Sir Henry

McMahon, the British High Commissioner in Egypt, had written to Sherif Hussein of Mecca: "We hereby confirm to you the declaration of Lord Kitchener...in which was manifested our desire for the independence of the Arab countries and their inhabitants, and our readiness to approve an Arab Caliphate upon its proclamation." Two months later McMahon wrote again to Hussein about the area that today corresponds to the Arabian Peninsula, Iraq, Syria, Lebanon, Jordan, and Palestine: "Great Britain is prepared to recognize and uphold the independence of the Arabs in all the regions lying within the frontiers proposed by the Sharif of Mecca."[51]

There was also a third aspect to the British deception. On January 3, 1916, the British had signed a secret agreement with the French. World War I was not yet over, but the Sykes-Picot Agreement had already divided the land among the victors. France would rule over Syria-Lebanon while Britain would rule over two provinces in Mesopotamia. Palestine would be subject to joint Anglo-French rule. In spite of its promises to both the Jews and the Arabs, Great Britain planned to govern the land.

Two additional ethical problems with the Balfour Declaration must be considered. First, the perceived need for a Jewish homeland arose from the anti-Semitism within European countries. Why was the solution to that problem not found in Europe itself? Why did British leaders look to a part of the world inhabited by non-Europeans? To put it simply, why were Arabs in Palestine asked to pay the price for European anti-Semitism?[52]

Second, what right did Great Britain have to make any promises about the land of Palestine in the first place? In November of 1917 the British had no authority whatsoever in Palestine. They did not consult the inhabitants of Palestine about their wishes; Britain unilaterally declared that a national home for the Jewish people should be established there. One writer summarized the famous declaration as "a document in which one nation solemnly promises to a second nation the country of a third nation."[53]

## THE 1948 WAR

Prior to the 1948 war, the United Nations Security Council voted to partition the land of Palestine into two separate states. Even though the Zionist leadership was disappointed that they were not granted more land, they eagerly embraced the possibility of statehood. After Israel declared its independence in the middle of May, the surrounding Arab nations immediately declared war on the new nation. According to the Israeli narrative, the new nation had to defend itself against five invading armies. There were 640,000 Israelis being threatened by 1,200,000 Arabs in Palestine and 80,000,000 Arabs in surrounding countries.

The odds against Israel were, however, not as great as those statistics make it appear. Israeli historian Benny Morris has described this picture of the 1948 war as "one of the most tenacious myths relating to 1948."[54]

| Nation | Troop Numbers Mid-May 1948 | Troop Strength Mid-July 1948 |
|---|---|---|
| Israel | 35,000 | 65,000 |
| 5 Arab Armies | 28,000 | 40,000 |

[55]

Morris summarizes: "It was superior Jewish firepower, manpower, organization, and command and control that determined the outcome of the battle."[56] Former Israeli Foreign Minister Shlomo Ben-Ami writes, "The invasion by the Arab armies did not necessarily mean that the Jews now faced superior Arab forces. The invading Arab armies were ill prepared for battle, and poorly equipped; they suffered from a total lack of co-ordination and very low motivation."[57] He elaborates: "It is certainly true that contrary to what the Zionists wanted us to believe when they propagated the myth about the Israeli David winning the day against the Arab Goliath.... Israel won the 1948 war so conclusively precisely because her forces were larger and better trained than the poorly equipped and ill-commanded armies of her enemies."[58]

## THE NAKBA

Israel had accepted the United Nations Security Council's decision to divide the land into two separate states, but the Arabs had emphatically rejected the partition because they believed it to be terribly unjust. Israel had by the Arabs' calculations been granted far more land than it deserved.

| States | Population prior to Partition | Land Ownership prior to Partition | Land Granted under Partition |
|---|---|---|---|
| Jewish state | 35% | 6.6% | 57% |
| Arab state | 65% | 87.5% | 43% |

[59 60]

Not only had Israel received a percentage of the land entirely out of proportion to the size of its population, it was also granted the most fertile land along the coast of the Mediterranean Sea, while the Arabs were given the less arable hill country. The oranges grown in the groves outside of the Arab city of Jaffa had been one of Palestine's trademarks for centuries, but now the city and the groves were to be in Israel's territory.[61] Fear of what the future might hold gripped the Arabs. Is it any surprise that they rejected the partition plan?

UN Resolution 181 was scheduled to take effect on May 15, 1948, dividing the land into two states, but the Zionists planned and carried out military actions months before that date. On March 10, they finalized Plan Dalet, which included a concise description of how the Arab population would be removed from Israel's territory:

> These operations can be carried out in the following manner: Either by destroying villages (by setting fire to them, by blowing them up, and by planting mines in their rubble), and especially those population centres that are difficult to control permanently; or by mounting combing and control operations according to the following guidelines: encirclement of the villages, conducting a search inside them. In case of resistance, the armed forces must be wiped out and the population expelled outside the border of the state.[62]

Hundreds of villages were emptied of their Arab inhabitants in what has become known as al-Nakba (Arabic for "the catastrophe"). The residents of those villages were expelled from their homes, resulting in 700,000 refugees.[63]

The most infamous example came with the village of Deir Yassin. In cooperation with the Haganah, the major Zionist paramilitary organization, two fiercely militant splinter militias called the Stern Gang and the Irgun attacked the village on April 9. The leadership of those two militias included two future Israeli prime ministers, Yitzhak Shamir and Menachem Begin. Between 100 and 110 inhabitants were massacred, including women and children. Morris describes the large-scale effect of the massacre:

...the news of what had happened—extensively covered and exaggerated in the Arab media for weeks—had a profoundly demoralizing effect on the Palestinian Arabs and was a major factor in their massive flight during the following weeks and months. The IDF [Israeli Defense Force] Intelligence Service called Deir Yassin "a decisive accelerating factor" in the general Arab exodus.[64]

Prior to the day that Israel declared its independence, the Zionist forces had already achieved the goal of ridding their land of most of its Arab residents. By May 15, 1948, an estimated 250,000 Palestinians had already become refugees.[65] According to David Ben-Gurion, "Until the British left, no Jewish settlement, however remote, was entered or seized by the Arabs, while the Haganah ... captured many Arab positions and liberated Tiberias and Haifa, Jaffa and Safad.... So, on the day of destiny [when Israel declared its independence], that part of Palestine where the Haganah could operate was almost clear of Arabs."[66]

During the truce in June of 1948, Ben-Gurion learned that Palestinians were trying to return to their homes. He gave the order to stop all such attempts.[67] Ben-Ami describes what happened:

> It was only after the practice [of denying refugees the ability to return] had been established by the army that, on 21 July 1948, a special decision by the Cabinet made this into *ex post facto* official policy. A month later, another Cabinet decision institutionalised the policy of inheriting the abandoned Arab villages and lands, and settling them with Jews. There was hardly any opposition in the government to this decision...
>
> And indeed, this, Israel's formal rejection of the refugees' claim for return—a position that remains intact to this day—rather than the expulsion and the dispossession, is the real defining moment of the conflict.[68]

The UN Security Council had appointed Count Folke Bernadotte, a member of the Swedish royal family, to serve as a special mediator during the June truce. In World War II he had served as president of the Swedish

Red Cross and had rescued Jews from the Nazis. In July 1948 a second truce was established. Bernadotte proposed that the land be redivided between the two states and that refugees be allowed to return to their homes. In his report to the UN, he laid out his case: "It would be an offense against the principles of elemental justice if these innocent victims of the conflict were denied the right to return to their homes, while Jewish immigrants flow into Palestine, and, indeed, at least offer the threat of permanent replacement of the Arab refugees who have been rooted in the land for centuries."[69] Bernadotte's plan was rejected by the Zionist leadership, and he was assassinated on September 17 by the Stern Gang.[70]

On December 11, 1948, the UN General Assembly passed Resolution 194. Paragraph 11 dealt directly with the problem of the refugees:

> The General Assembly, having considered further the situation in Palestine.... Resolves that the refugees wishing to return to their homes and live at peace with their neighbours should be permitted to do so at the earliest practicable date, and that compensation should be paid for the property of those choosing not to return and for loss of or damage to property which, under principles of international law or in equity, should be made good by the Governments or authorities responsible.[71]

On November 29, 1947, the Zionist leaders had eagerly embraced UN Resolution 181's proposal that Israel be established as a state. Twelve months later they flatly rejected the UN's later resolution to deal with the huge refugee problem that Israel's creation had produced and which remains to the present time. American rabbi Michael Lerner comments, "Israelis who argue that the 1947 partition plan was legitimate and that Palestinians had a moral obligation to accept the division of their land ordained by the United Nations are usually inconsistent when it comes to their own obligation to live by subsequent resolutions of the United Nations."[72]

Israel refused to take responsibility for the 700,000 men, women, and children forced from their homes in the Nakba. In 1953 the Israeli government published an official pamphlet claiming that the Palestinians had been ordered to leave their homes and flee their villages by express commands coming over the radio from Arab authorities. According to Israel, the reasoning behind the evacuation orders was that the empty villages would allow the Arab forces the opportunity to defeat the Zionist forces.[73]

Historians debate the precise reason the Arabs fled their villages.[74] Benny Morris says that a share of the blame belongs to poor Arab leadership but concludes, "Above all, let me reiterate, the refugee problem was caused by attacks by Jewish forces on Arab villages and towns and by the inhabitants' fear of such attacks compounded by expulsions, atrocities and rumors of atrocities—and by the crucial Israeli Cabinet decision in June 1948 to bar a refugee return."[75]

Israel lost no time in destroying villages or resettling them with Jewish immigrants. This resulted in the refugees being unable to return to their homes and the evidence of their history in the land being destroyed. Israeli general Moshe Dayan acknowledged this in 1949: "Jewish villages were built in the place of Arab villages. You don't even know the names of these Arab villages, and I don't blame you, because these geography books no longer exist. Not only do the books not exist, the Arab villages are not there either.... There is not one single place built in this country that did not have a former Arab population."[76]

Shlomo Ben-Ami acknowledges what actually took place in the Nakba. "The reality on the ground...was that of an Arab community in a state of terror facing a ruthless Israeli army whose path to victory was paved not only by its exploits against the regular Arab armies, but also by the intimidation, and at times atrocities and massacres, it perpetrated against the civilian Arab community."[77]

## THE 1967 WAR

After the seizure of Palestinian land in the Nakba, the next major turning point for the Palestinians was the war in 1967. The Israelis won a decisive victory over Egypt, Jordan, and Syria. The war is often presented as a preemptive strike taken in response to threats from Egypt's Nasser, but Israeli officials have acknowledged that Egypt was not a serious threat to Israel's security. Yitzhak Rabin, the chief of staff in the Israeli Defense Forces in 1967, said, "I do not believe that Nasser wanted war. The two divisions he sent into Sinai on May 14 would not have been enough to unleash an offensive against Israel. He knew it and we knew it."[78] Former Prime Minister Menachem Begin was even more direct: "In June 1967 we again had a choice. The Egyptian army concentrations in the Sinai approaches do not prove that Nasser was really about to attack us. We must be honest with ourselves. We decided to attack him."[79]

The 1967 war resulted in Israel's occupation of East Jerusalem, the West Bank, and the Gaza Strip. UN Security Council Resolution 242 was passed on November 22, 1967. In spite of its call for the "withdrawal of Israeli armed forces from territories occupied in the recent conflict," the occupation continues to the present day.

Within weeks following the conclusion of the war, settlements started to be built in the conquered territories. Prime Minister Levi Eshkol asked Theodore Meron, the foreign minister's legal counsel and the government's top authority on international law, whether such settlements were legal. Meron responded unambiguously in writing: "My conclusion is that civilian settlement in the administered territories contravenes explicit provisions of the Fourth Geneva Convention." He cited Article 49, paragraph 6: "The Occupying Power shall not deport or transfer parts of its own civilian population into the territories it occupies."[80] With 540,000 Israelis now living in East Jerusalem and the West Bank, it is obvious that the Israeli government chose not to follow its legal counsel's advice.

Some aspects of Palestinian life in the West Bank did improve under Israeli control. Benny Morris points out, however, that such improvements are not the whole story.

> But none of this sufficed to erase—though it may for a time have tempered—the inhabitants' political frustration and anger of their feelings of discrimination and inequality compared with the Israelis. Moreover, despite the average increases in income and living standards, vast pockets of abject poverty continued to exist and grow...
>
> With the population exploding, land and water resources were shrinking: By 1987 the 2,500 Israeli settlers in the Strip—or 0.4 percent of the territory's total population—had control over some 28 percent of its state lands. Similarly, much of the underground

## The Palestinian Narrative

water reserves, in both territories, were diverted to the use of Israel itself or Jewish settlers. On average, West Bank settlers used twelve times as much water as did Palestinians. The amount of irrigated Arab land in the West Bank declined by 30 percent between 1967 and 1987.[81]

For over forty-five years now, Palestinians have been living under the control of Israel. Morris describes what that has meant to the Palestinians:

> Israelis liked to believe, and tell the world, that they were running an "enlightened" or "benign" occupation, qualitatively different from other military occupations the world had seen. The truth was radically different. Like all occupations, Israel's was founded on brute force, repression and fear, collaboration and treachery, beatings and torture chambers, and daily intimidation, humiliation, and manipulation....
>
> Military administration, uncurbed by the civil rights considerations that applied in Israel, possessed ample measures to suppress dissidence and protest. These included curfews; house arrest, with resulting loss of wages; judicial proceedings, ending in prison terms or fines—the work of the military courts in the territories, and the Supreme Court which backed them, will surely go down as a dark age in the annals of Israel's judicial system—or expulsions; administrative detentions, or imprisonment without trial, for renewable six-month terms; and commercial and school shutdowns, usually in response to shopkeepers' strikes or disturbances by students.[82]

## Peace Efforts

The Declaration of Principles contained in the 1993 Oslo Accords promised a Palestinian state within five years, but those promises proved to be an illusion. American rabbi Michael Lerner describes the results of the accords:

> In the first phase of the implementation of Oslo, Israeli troops were withdrawn from major Palestinian cities. From Israel's standpoint,

this, together with the creation of a Palestinian Authority democratically elected to run the new system was a major benefit to the Palestinian people....

Yet this was a long way from what Palestinians wanted: Independence as a separate country with its own borders, its own representative in the United Nations, and its own ability to participate in international affairs....

Implementing Oslo involved the creation of different zones in the West Bank, and to go from one zone to another Palestinians found themselves standing in long lines, sometimes for hours, to get from one town to another....

The decision to respond to acts of terror by the then-still-marginal Hamas by punishing the entire Palestinian people proved to many Palestinians that they were still being treated as "the enemy," not as a friend who had just signed a peace treaty. The collective punishments involved closing the borders between Israel and Palestine. This effectively prevented many Palestinians from being able to work in Israel or to engage in trade with Israel.[83]

The Camp David meeting in 2000 was equally ineffective in bringing any substantial or lasting change. Even though Prime Minister Ehud Barak offered Yasser Arafat what was characterized as a generous offer, nothing was done to resolve the future of Palestinian refugees. King Abdullah II of Jordan summarizes the problem:

> Barak presented a package that represented an advance on any previous Israeli proposal, but for the Palestinian negotiators it fell short. Under his proposals, Israel would permanently retain over 10 percent of the West Bank and would control a further 10 percent for a period of twenty years. The return of refugees was treated in the context of a family reunification program and excluded the issue of the Palestinian right of return (the right of Palestinians who were evicted or fled in 1948 and 1967 to return to their homes).[84]

Furthermore, Israel's control over daily life in the West Bank would have continued. Lerner writes:

> Israel planned to retain military roads that crisscrossed the new Palestinian state and checkpoints that would have made passage from one part of the Palestinian state to another very difficult. Imagine this from the standpoint of the Palestinians. It was like someone who occupies your home offering to return 90 percent of it but insisting on retaining control of the hallways; you'd need permission whenever you wanted to go from one part of your house to another.[85]

In March of 2002 at a summit meeting in Beirut, Lebanon, Saudi Crown Prince Abdullah proposed a peace plan to the twenty-two members of the Arab League. The league formally approved the eight-point Saudi Peace Initiative. The proposal included the Arab countries' affirmation to "consider the Arab-Israeli conflict ended, and enter into a peace agreement with Israel, and provide security for all the states of the region." It requested Israel to affirm the "full Israeli withdrawal from all territories occupied since 1967... [and] achievement of a just solution to the Palestinian Refugee problem to be agreed upon in accordance with the UN General Assembly Resolution 194."[86] In June of that year the fifty-seven members of the Council of Foreign Ministers of the Organization of the Islamic Conference (OIC) met in Sudan and endorsed the peace initiative.[87] It also received the endorsement of Yassar Arafat, US Secretary of State Colin Powell, and Israeli Foreign Minister Shimon Peres.[88] The peace initiative provided a genuine opportunity for negotiated progress toward peace. Israeli historian Avi Shlaim explains the importance of the proposal and the Israeli government's response:

> The significance of the plan lay in the offer to Israel of peace not only with its immediate neighbors but peace and normal relations with the whole Arab world: it marked a major watershed in the evolution of Arab policy toward Israel....
> The Israeli response to this profound change in Arab politics was worse than rejection: it was complete indifference. The offer

to recognize Israel within its pre-1967 borders was treated by [Israeli Prime Minister] Ariel Sharon not as an opportunity for a diplomatic breakthrough but as an irrelevance.[89]

In spite of Israel's response, the 2007 Summit Conference of the Arab League in Riyadh, Saudi Arabia, reaffirmed it unanimously.

The Arab Peace Initiative does not, of course, solve every problem; serious negotiations on substantive issues would still be required. But the initiative does constitute a reversal of the Three Nos issued at the 1967 Khartoum Conference and reflects a genuine willingness by the Arab states to seek a workable solution.

Naomi Chazan, former deputy speaker of the Israeli Knesset, calls the Arab Peace Initiative "the most strategic and hopeful framework for comprehensive solution to the Arab-Israel conflict." Yet the Israeli government's response has continued to be lukewarm if not entirely indifferent.[90] Why is Israel ignoring such an opportunity to make progress toward peace—a peace they repeatedly swear that they want?

## Is the World Aware?

Dawoud El-Alami, who was born in Jerusalem and educated in Egypt, summarizes what many Palestinians feel:

> From a Palestinian perspective it seems that Israelis, non-Israeli Jews and indeed the world are oblivious to or simply do not care about what has been done to the Palestinians. How can the Jewish people, whether in the Holy Land or elsewhere, a people themselves so badly wronged within living memory, in conscience accept that the creation of the Jewish state has been achieved by the displacement and the continued agony of another people?...
> 
> Why does a colonial state declared by a conquering people have full rights before the United Nations, while the original population of the land that it has usurped is deprived of any right of statehood and, in the struggle for equal treatment and gradually worn down over the years, is ultimately forced to beg for the minimum of what is expected by any other people.[91]

## The Palestinian Narrative

The Palestinian narrative outlined in this chapter amply demonstrates that there is another perspective that must be heard. Americans need to understand that Zionist leaders starting with Theodore Herzl himself knew that their desire for a homeland would create serious problems with the Arab population already living in the land. The famous Balfour Declaration, which is regularly cited as the legal basis for Israel's existence, was deceptive and unethical. The 1948 war between Israel and its Arab neighbors must not be reduced and simplified into a battle between a modern David and an Arab Goliath. Lasting injustices resulted from the wars of 1948 and 1967. Americans should also learn about the attempts that Arab leaders have made to come to a negotiated settlement that would safeguard Israel's existence as well as address those injustices that Palestinians have been experiencing for decades.

Americans' lack of knowledge of the Palestinian narrative is tragic. Such historical ignorance cannot help but skew our approach to the Israeli-Palestinian conflict. But even more regrettable is how little Americans know about what is happening now in Palestine and Israel. That is the subject to be examined in the next chapter.

## Chapter Three
# The Present Situation

*To crush underfoot
all prisoners in the land,
to deny people their rights
before the Most High,
to deprive them of justice—
would not the Lord see such things?*

LAMENTATIONS 3:34–35

WHEN I LEARNED THAT A COUPLE FROM OUR CHURCH was going on a tour of the Holy Land, I urged them to take special note of the Separation Barrier, the tall and lengthy wall that separates Israel from the West Bank. I told them that I hoped to hear what they thought about it after they got back.

Upon their return I asked the couple about their impression of the wall. The man looked at me somewhat quizzically and then hesitantly said, "What wall are you talking about? We didn't see any wall."

I was astounded at his answer and quickly asked, "Did you go to Bethlehem? Didn't you have to pass through the wall to get there from Jerusalem?"

"Oh, that wall," he said. "Yes, we did see a wall when we went to Bethlehem, but our guide didn't say anything about it. Is that the wall you were talking about?"

## Where Do We Go from Here?

As that conversation demonstrates, many Americans—including Christians who go on a tour of the Holy Land—know little of what is going on in Palestine and Israel today. Tourists return home with increased knowledge of Bible history and with a glowing impression of modern Israel, but they learn little, if anything, about the lives of Palestinians. Quick trips into the West Bank may be made in order to visit Bethlehem and Jericho, but contact with individual Palestinians—including believers in Christ—does not take place.[92]

The Israeli and Palestinian narratives of the two previous chapters could be easily expanded and the significance of those narratives endlessly debated. Attempts could be made to compare the injustices of the Holocaust and the Nakba. But that thorny issue will never be settled.

What can be agreed upon is that the Jews and the Palestinians have both been mistreated by other nations over the course of the last one hundred years. Both groups of people are also guilty of mistreating each other. Former Israeli Foreign Minister Shlomo Ben-Ami summarizes the challenge of drawing conclusions from the historical material.

> No one in this conflict has a monopoly on suffering and martyrdom; nor is the responsibility for war atrocities exclusive to one party. In this tragic tribal dispute, both Jews and Arabs have committed acts of unpardonable violence, and both have succumbed at times to their most bestial instincts. What is no less grave is that they have both too frequently chosen the wrong course, refusing to see the changing realities and adapt their policies accordingly.[93]

Listening to the history contained in the Israeli and Palestinian narratives is important, but eventually an examination of the present needs to be undertaken. What is happening in the land now?

In Deuteronomy 19:16–18a, Moses gave the Israelites instructions on how to handle accusations of injustice. They were not to jump to conclusions. "If a malicious witness takes the stand to accuse someone of a crime … the judges must make a thorough investigation."

## The Present Situation

Such an investigation is also necessary today. On the one hand, Israeli politicians stress the freedom that Arab citizens of their nation enjoy, and they also emphasize the security threats that Israelis must continually endure. On the other hand, charges of gross injustice are still leveled today over Israel's treatment of Palestinians. What are the grounds for those accusations? What is happening in Israel and Palestine today?

## Life in Israel

Israeli politicians take pride in pointing out that the nation of Israel is a democracy. For example, during the Arab Spring of 2011, Israeli Prime Minister Benjamin Netanyahu emphasized Israel's democracy when he spoke to the US Congress:

> My friends, you don't need to do nation building in Israel. We're already built. You don't need to export democracy to Israel. We've already got it....
>
> Courageous Arab protesters [in other countries] are now struggling to secure these very same rights for their peoples, for their societies. We're proud that over one million Arab citizens of Israel have been enjoying these rights for decades. Of the 300 million Arabs in the Middle East and North Africa, only Israel's Arab citizens enjoy real democratic rights.[94]

Evidence of those democratic rights can be cited. For example, the Palestinian citizens of Israel elected seventeen Arab members to the Knesset in 2015. More importantly, the 1948 Israeli Declaration of Independence guarantees equality.

> THE STATE OF ISRAEL will be open for Jewish immigration and for the Ingathering of the Exiles; it will foster the development of the country *for the benefit of all its inhabitants*; it will be based on freedom, justice and peace as envisaged by the prophets of Israel; *it will ensure complete equality of social and political rights to all its inhabitants irrespective of religion, race or sex*; it will guarantee freedom of religion, conscience, language, education and culture; it

will safeguard the Holy Places of all religions; and it will be faithful to the principles of the Charter of the United Nations. (emphasis added)

It certainly appears that Israel is a democracy just like the United States is, but given the frequent charges of injustice against Palestinians, more investigation is needed.

Israeli politicians frequently refer to Israel not just as a democracy but as a "Jewish nation." To Americans those two words convey the ideas that Israel contains a lot of Jewish people and that it was created to protect Jewish people from anti-Semitic persecution. But there is more to the term "Jewish nation" than Americans assume.

In Israel, citizenship is not the same as nationality. To Americans that is a concept that is hard to grasp because someone who is a citizen of the United States is also an American. But in Israel this is not the case. As strange as it may sound, there is no such thing as Israeli nationality. In 1972 the Israeli High Court ruled that "there is no such thing as an Israeli nation separate from the Jewish people." There is an Israeli nation but not an Israeli nationality. Israel recognizes 140 different nationalities among the citizens of its nation. Those nationalities include Russian, Polish, French, Arab, and of course, Jewish.

The Law of Return of 1950 states that Jews from any part of the world can come to Israel and become citizens because they already possess Jewish nationality. But Palestinians who were born in the land are denied citizenship if they fled the country for even a short time during the 1948 war. Palestinians born in the land to families who have lived there for centuries have no guaranteed legal status, but Jewish people who have never set foot in the land have an open invitation to become citizens.[95]

Even the Arabs who do have Israeli citizenship have fewer rights than Jewish citizens. In Israel, "rights of citizenship" are less legally significant than "rights of nationality" because Israeli citizenship is secondary to Jewish nationality. As a Jewish nation, Israel exists for Jews and not for all of its citizens.

Prime Minister Netanyahu regularly mentions the Palestinians' refusal to accept Israel as a Jewish state. (See the second paragraph of Netanyahu's

## The Present Situation

quotation at the end of chapter 1). To Americans it sounds like he is making such a simple and reasonable request—but that is because we miss the full significance of the term "Jewish state." When Netanyahu insists on the Palestinians' recognition of Israel as a "Jewish state," he is actually demanding that Israel be recognized as existing for Jews and not for anyone else. No Arab leader will meet that demand because it would in effect be an agreement that the Palestinian citizens of Israel, who make up 20 percent of the population, should not have the same legal status as the Jewish citizens of Israel. Netanyahu's terminology hides the audacity of his demand. When Egypt signed a peace treaty with Israel in 1979 and Jordan signed one in 1994, there was no demand for recognizing Israel as a "Jewish state." Even in 1993 when the PLO's Yasser Arafat formally recognized Israel's right to exist, there was no use of that terminology. But now Netanyahu is demanding that one out of every five of the citizens of Israel be officially demoted to second-class standing.

The priority of nationality over citizenship means that Jewish people have rights that are denied the non-Jewish citizens of Israel. What are some of these rights?

LAND USE. Palestinian citizens of Israel do not enjoy the same access to land as Jewish citizens of the country. Today the Israel Lands Administration oversees 93 percent of all Israeli land. Policy is made by the twenty-two-member Israel Land Council, which is composed of representatives of twelve Israeli government ministers and ten members of the Jewish National Fund (JNF).

The JNF was established long before Israel became a nation. Its purpose was to raise money to purchase land that would be used by Jews to establish Jewish communities and farms. In a 2004 court case, the JNF described itself as "not a public body that works for the benefit of all citizens of the state. The loyalty of the JNF is given to the Jewish people and only to them is the JNF obligated. The JNF, as the owner of the JNF land, does not have a duty to practice equality towards all citizens of the state."[96] With such a large JNF representation on the Israel Land Administration, is it surprising that Palestinian citizens of Israel lack the same access to land that Jewish citizens enjoy?

The Absentee Property Law of 1950 promotes further discrimination.

As already stated, Arabs who lived in the land prior to the 1948 war but who fled from the land during the war were not allowed to return home, and they were not compensated for their homes. Meron Benvenisti, who served as deputy mayor of Jerusalem from 1971 to 1978, describes how even the land owned by Arabs who did not flee their villages was taken over by Israelis:

> This was accomplished in a simple and not overly delicate manner: first the land would be declared "a closed area," where Arabs were barred from entering the plots they had under cultivation, making it impossible for them to tend them. Then the minister of agriculture would, in accordance with the regulations, send "warnings" to the Arab farmers, informing them that if they did not cultivate their landholdings, these would be classified as fallow. Since the Arabs were prevented by the closure orders from working their land, it was in due course declared "fallow," and the minister would then transfer it to Jewish farmers.[97]

If the taking of Arab land by this process had only taken place in the past, it would be another historical event to be grieved. But according to the B'Tselem, an Israeli civil rights group, similar procedures are being used today to take Palestinian land in the West Bank.[98] The process is technically legal but terribly unjust.

What about Palestinians who left their homes after November 1947—perhaps for a period as short as one day—but remained within the borders of what became Israel following the war? According to the law, those people became "present absentees," meaning that they were present in the nation but absent from their homes. They too were unable to return to their homes or be compensated for them. Today one in four Arab citizens is a "present absentee."[99]

The Planning and Building Law of 1965 determined which villages would be categorized as "official villages" within the land. Arab villages that did not receive that designation receive no government services today. Homes in those villages are not connected to the national power grid or water supply. Neither do they have state schools or post offices. Those villages also have no authority to grant building permits to their residents. Not having a building permit means that homes are subject to demolition; the Israeli government can destroy them at any time because they are legally classified as being on state land. Home demolitions are often carried out at night with just a few minutes of advance notice. There is no time to salvage the contents of the house. Between 1995 and 1999, almost four hundred houses were demolished in unrecognized villages.[100]

In seven hundred towns in Israel (70 percent of all Israeli towns), admission committees establish criteria for who can live there. The committees can filter out those who are deemed "unsuitable" for the "social fabric" of the community. That legal provision allows for Palestinian citizens of Israel to be excluded from purchasing homes. The attitude of the admission committees is so well known that Palestinians do not even apply.[101]

MARITAL LAW. Marriages for Palestinian citizens of Israel also have legal limitations. The Nationality and Entry into Israel Law, passed in 2003, restricts Palestinian and even Jewish citizens from marrying Palestinians from the West Bank. If such a marriage takes place, the West Bank spouse cannot become a citizen or even a resident of Israel. This law is not based on any potential risk that an individual may pose for security but solely on ethnic origin.[102]

EDUCATIONAL OPPORTUNITY. Education is yet another area where preference is given to Jewish citizens. The nation's annual investment in a Jewish student ages 5–15 is $428; the investment in a Palestinian student of the same age is just $128.[103]

SOCIAL SERVICES. What kind of social services are available for the Palestinian citizens of Israel? In 2008 Palestinian citizens made up 20 percent of the population. The percentage of the government's total development budget that was allocated for those citizens amounted to only 4 percent even though half of all Arab families live in poverty.[104]

Criticism of Israel's treatment of its Palestinian citizens comes not just from Arab or foreign sources. The Orr Commission was established by the Israeli government to investigate the events of October 2000 in which twelve Arab citizens, one Jewish citizen, and one resident of Gaza were killed. The commission was headed by Theodore Orr, a justice on Israel's Supreme Court. The official summation of the report did not clear Arab leadership of all responsibility for the deaths, but it did confirm the ingrained discrimination that Palestinian citizens of Israel face:

> The events, their unusual character and serious results were the consequence of deep-seated factors that created an explosive situation in the Israeli Arab population. The state and generations of its government failed in a lack of comprehensive and deep handling of the serious problems created by the existence of a large Arab minority inside the Jewish state.
>
> Government handling of the Arab sector has been primarily neglectful and discriminatory. The establishment did not show sufficient sensitivity to the needs of the Arab population, and did not take enough action in order to allocate state resources in an equal manner. The state did not do enough or try hard enough to create equality for its Arab citizens or to uproot discriminatory or unjust phenomenon. Meanwhile, not enough was done to enforce the law in the Arab sector, and the illegal and undesirable phenomena that took root there.
>
> As a result of this and other processes, serious distress prevailed in the Arab sector in various areas. Evidence of the distress included poverty, unemployment, a shortage of land, serious problems in the education system and substantially defective infrastructure. These all contributed to on-going ferment that increased leading up to October 2000 and constituted a fundamental contribution to the outbreak of the events.[105]

The Orr Commission described the situation in 2000, but life for the Palestinian citizens of Israel has not substantially changed since then. Israel is a democracy in name only.

## Life in the West Bank

Investigating life within Israel reveals patterns of discrimination against its Palestinian citizenry, but an investigation of life in the occupied West Bank reveals even more serious patterns of discrimination.

DIVIDED GOVERNANCE. In the Oslo Accords of 1993, the West

## The Present Situation

Bank was divided into three distinct areas in which civil jurisdiction and security control were divided between Israel and the Palestinian Authority. These areas were created as temporary measures that were intended to lead within five years to the establishment of a Palestinian state, but only small changes have taken place over the last twenty years.

| Area | Civil Jurisdiction | Security Control | % of West Bank Land in 1993 | % of West Bank Land in 2012 |
|---|---|---|---|---|
| A | Palestinian Authority | Palestinian Authority | 3 | 17 |
| B | Palestinian Authority | Israel | 24 | 24 |
| C | Israel | Israel | 73 | 59 |

106

Areas A and B include most of the Palestinian population centers and over 2,400,000 people, but those two areas are subdivided into 165 isolated units of land that have no territorial contiguity and are surrounded by Area C.[107] This division of land gives Israel the power to control the movement of the people into and out of Areas A and B.

The United Nations Office for the Coordination of Humanitarian Affairs (OCHA) published a fact sheet in September 2011 filled with statistics about the limitations that Palestinians in the West Bank face. The Palestinians' access to any of their own land that borders on fifty-five Israeli settlements is restricted. Imagine owning land but not being allowed to set foot on it.

Israeli settlers living in the West Bank can travel on roads that are reserved for their use alone; Palestinians cannot use them. Due to

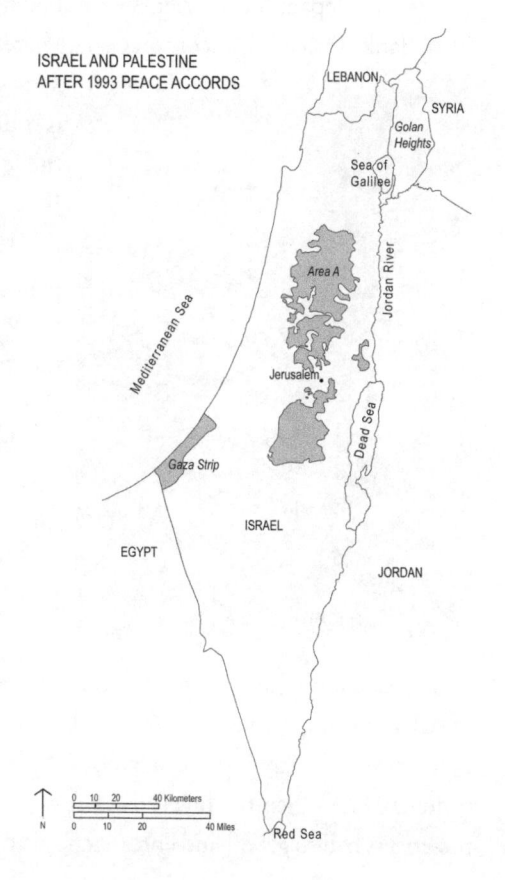

Israeli checkpoints and roadblocks, there are approximately 200,000 people living in seventy different villages who are forced to use detours in order to travel to other West Bank villages; these detours make their trips two to five times longer than if they were allowed to use the direct route to their destinations. Imagine what it would be like to have your travel time doubled or tripled every time you made the effort to visit a relative in a nearby city.[108]

ACCESS BARRIER. Movement between the West Bank and Israel is also severely restricted due to the Separation Barrier, which was constructed beginning in 2002. The barrier is made of concrete walls, fences, ditches, razor wire, groomed paths, an electronic monitoring system, patrol roads, and a buffer zone that ranges from 500 to 2,500 feet wide on the Palestinian side of the barrier. It is this wall that my American friends failed to "notice" on their trip to Israel.

Yet the Separation Barrier does not actually separate Israel from the West Bank. Instead, it incorporates large areas of Palestinian land in the West Bank *into* Israel. The barrier is 440 miles long, which is twice the length of the border between Israel and the West Bank prior to the 1967 war. Approximately 85 percent of the barrier runs inside the West Bank so that Israeli settlements are not stranded on the Palestinian side. Imagine your neighbor constructing a wall between your adjacent properties but not consulting you about it and building 85 percent of it on land that is legally yours.[109]

Passing through a checkpoint in the Separation Barrier can take hours and be a humiliating experience. I once had the opportunity to get a small taste of what Palestinians regularly experience at checkpoints. On a Sunday evening I took a bus from Ramallah to Jerusalem. When the bus arrived at the Qalandiya checkpoint, all the passengers had to get off and enter a fenced-in area where we waited for our turn to go through the turnstile. My fellow passengers were tired and longing to get to their destinations. They crowded toward the turnstile so they could get through as quickly as possible. Since I was a tourist, I decided to let the others go in front of me. I was not going to push my way to the front. But soon another bus arrived, and I realized that if I was going to get through the checkpoint at all, I had to follow the example of the other passengers.

Every time an inch of space opened up in front of me, I moved my foot or arm forward. When I had maneuvered my way to the front and was standing right at the turnstile, the checkpoint guard electronically shut it down. As I waited for it to become operational again, I felt squeezed between the metal bars of the turnstile and the body of the person directly behind me.

A couple of minutes later I was allowed through. I presented my backpack for inspection and walked through the metal detector. Then I went to the window where an Israeli soldier was seated. I showed my United States passport, but she barked that I was showing her the wrong page. As quickly as possible, I found the correct page, and to my relief she waved me on. My experience at the checkpoint was annoying but educational. I could only imagine what the hassle and humiliation of going through a checkpoint every day along with hundreds of other people would be like.

B'Tselem, an Israeli civil rights group, recorded what took place at one checkpoint in July of 2013 starting at 2:00 in the morning.

> At that time, some fifty laborers were already waiting in line. Less than a quarter of an hour later, hundreds more had arrived. B'Tselem spoke to the laborers, and they described how the checkpoint operates. They explained that crossing it takes so long because there are only two metal detectors in place, and inspections are lengthy. On Sunday, when the checkpoint is particularly busy, all eight inspection stations are open, but on other weekdays only four are usually staffed. After the laborers pass through the metal detector, guards

randomly choose some laborers for further inspection. The further inspection is conducted individually. Each laborer enters a room and must strip down to his underwear in front of a guard. After putting their clothes back on, they are taken to a small room, where they have to wait until eight laborers have gathered, and only then are they sent on to the regular inspection stations.[110]

According to a United Nations OCHA report in July 2012, the Separation Barrier creates severe limitations for Palestinians who own farmland on the Israeli side of the barrier. They can only get to their land by first receiving a permit to pass through the barrier. During the 2011 harvest, about 42 percent of the applications for permits were rejected. If a permit was acquired, the Palestinian farmer had to pass through one of the eighty gates designated for access to agricultural land, but most of those gates were open for just a limited period of time each day.

The OCHA report also included information from an Israeli government document which estimated that fifteen thousand West Bank Palestinian day laborers smuggled themselves into Israel every day because they could not acquire the necessary travel permits.[111] That observation deserves special attention because Israel's official purpose in building the Separation Barrier was to stop suicide bombers from entering Israel from the West Bank. The wall has frequently been given credit for accomplishing that goal, but Israel's acknowledgement that fifteen thousand people slip through the barrier each day calls that claim into question. If thousands of people can smuggle themselves every day through the wall, then suicide bombers could certainly enter Israel. Furthermore, Shin Bet, Israel's internal security service, acknowledged in 2006 that the main reason for the sharp decline in terrorist activity from 2002 to 2005 was not the Separation Barrier. It reported that the drop in suicide bombings was largely due instead to the cease-fire called by Hamas.[112]

One additional aspect of the Separation Barrier needs to be understood. The International Court of Justice, which is authorized by the United Nations and located in the Hague, issued an Advisory Opinion in 2004 declaring that the sections of the Separation Barrier that run inside the West Bank, along with the associated gate-and-permit regime, violate Israel's obligations under international law.[113] That legal opinion, however, did not stop

Israel from continuing the construction of the barrier.

ISRAELI SETTLEMENTS. As serious as the problems created by the Separation Barrier are, they are not as substantial as those connected to the Israeli settlements in the West Bank. According to Article 49 of the Fourth Geneva Convention, "The Occupying Power shall not deport or transfer parts of its own civilian population into the territory it occupies."

Israel maintains the Geneva Convention does not apply. The West Bank should be called "disputed territory" rather than "occupied territory" because of Jordan's previous claim to that land. But the international community generally does not accept that line of reasoning and believes that Israel's occupation is illegal. According to the Congressional Research Service, US policy on the settlements has varied since 1967.

> Until the 1980s, multiple Administrations either stated or implied that settlements were "contrary to international law," with President Carter's Secretary of State Cyrus Vance stating explicitly that settlements were "illegal" in 1980. President Reagan later stated that settlements were "not illegal," but "ill-advised" and "unnecessarily provocative." Since then, the executive branch has generally refrained from pronouncements on the settlements' legality. A common U.S. stance has been that settlements are an "obstacle to peace."[114]

Nevertheless, Israelis have built settlements in the West Bank, and the government has provided ongoing legal justification and protection for those settlements. Over the last forty-five years the settlements have continually grown in number and population.

| Year | Number of Settlements | Number of Settlers |
| --- | --- | --- |
| 1967 | 1 | No figures available |
| 1974 | 14 | No figures available |
| 1981 | 68 | 16,200 |
| 1988 | 110 | 63,600 |
| 1995 | 120 | 127,900 |
| 2002 | 123 | 211,416 |
| 2009 | 121 | 301,200 |
| 2014 | 135 | 340,000 |

[115] [116]

The figures above do not include East Jerusalem, which Israel annexed in 1967 in violation of international law. The estimated number of Israelis who have moved into East Jerusalem number 200,000.[117] That brings the total of Israeli settlers currently living on land that was supposed to be part of a Palestinian state in accordance with the Oslo Accords to 540,000.

The Israeli settlements have created major humanitarian concerns. A December 2012 report from the UN's OCHA observed that the annual average rate of growth in the settlements (excluding East Jerusalem) for the previous ten years was 5.3 percent. That compared to only a 1.8 percent growth rate for the Israeli population as a whole. Furthermore, about 80 percent of the settlers live on land that is on the Israeli side of the Separation Barrier. In effect, those settlements have been taken from the Palestinians and annexed to Israel. As the settlements grow, the Palestinians are being increasingly squeezed out of the land that Israel agreed would be part of the Palestinian state in the 1993 Oslo Accords.[118]

In March 2012, I had the opportunity to see for myself an example of the Israeli settlers' relentless desire for Palestinian land. South of Bethlehem is Daher's Vineyard. This farm is located in Area C, the area of the West Bank that is under Israel's civil and military control. The bus taking our group to the farm could not drive up to the gate because huge boulders had been placed on the road in order to block access. As we walked up the hill, we could see the modern Israeli settlements on all of the hills surrounding the farm.

Once inside, we were led to a cave where we were told about the history of the farm. Daher Nasser bought the land in 1916. Unlike many farmers in the area, the Nasser family has legal documentation of their ownership. Their paperwork provides proof of their ownership of the land during the Ottoman Empire, the British Mandate, the Jordanian rule, and the Israeli occupation. In spite of that documentation, the surrounding Israeli settlers have been trying to remove this Palestinian family from their land.

In 1991 the Israeli government declared the area to be state land, but the Nassers fought that claim in the courts. Ten years later the local council of Israeli settlements decided to build a road through the east side of the farm. That too was challenged, and the construction stopped. The council tried to build a road through the west side of the property in 2002, but the courts again intervened.

## The Present Situation

So far the Nassers have been able to hold on to their land—at a cost of $170,000 in legal fees. But harassment continues. The road to the farm has been blocked twice with boulders. Because they are denied the right to construct any more buildings, they have to meet with visitors in a cave. They never know when or how the next legal battle will come.

Early in 2012 a document was "delivered" to the family informing them that they no longer had legal permission to cultivate their land. The requirements for legal delivery were officially met because the document had been placed somewhere on the family's property, but if a family member had not stumbled across it in a field, the Nassers would not have had the necessary time to challenge the decision in court. On the morning of May 19, 2014, a bulldozer guarded by Israeli soldiers uprooted more than fifteen hundred apricot and apple trees in Daher's Vineyard, even though an appeal had been filed just a week before stating that the family could prove the trees had been planted on land owned by the family.

For the Nassers, access to water is also restricted. The family has been denied permission to dig wells; instead, rainwater has to be collected in cisterns. I remember standing in the farm and looking across at the Israeli settlements. The Nasser family is denied water needed to irrigate their crops while the Israelis just across the valley enjoy their swimming pools.

Learning about the constant oppression of the Nasser family is depressing, but my visit to Daher's Vineyard also had its inspiring side. The Nassers are believers in Christ who are trying to live out Jesus's instruction to "love your enemies." They do not hate the Israeli settlers. In fact, painted on a rock outside the gate is the family's motto: "We Refuse to Be Enemies."[119]

WATER ACCESS. As the story of Daher's Vineyard demonstrates, water consumption is a major issue in the West Bank. The World Health Organization recommends one hundred liters per person per day, but Palestinians are restricted in their access to water to a level far below this. Israelis consume an average of 350 liters of water per person per day, but Palestinians in the occupied territories consume only sixty liters per person per day.[120]

SETTLER VIOLENCE. Another serious area of concern comes from violence by Israeli settlers. The OHCA reports:

> The failure to respect international law, along with the lack of adequate law enforcement vis-à-vis settler violence and takeover of land has led to a state of impunity, which encourages further violence and undermines the physical security and livelihoods of Palestinians. Those demonstrating against settlement expansion or access restrictions imposed for the benefit of settlements (including the Barrier) are regularly subject to arrest or injury by Israeli forces.
>
> Israeli civil law is *de facto* applied to all settlers and settlements across the occupied West Bank, while Israeli military law is applied to Palestinians, except in East Jerusalem, which was illegally annexed to Israel. As a result, two separate legal systems and sets of rights are applied by the same authority in the same area, depending on the national origin of the persons, thereby discriminating against Palestinians.[121]

ADMINISTRATIVE DETENTION. The existence of two different legal systems allows for the practice of administrative detention. Palestinians can be picked up and held in jail or prison without being officially charged with a crime, without legal defense being allowed, and without any indication of how long their detention will last. As of October 2014, 473 Palestinians were being held in administrative detention. Some of them had been held for as long as two years.[122]

HOME DEMOLITION. An additional issue comes from Israel's practice of home demolition in the West Bank. The Fourth Geneva Convention prohibits the "destruction by the Occupying Power of real or personal property belonging individually or collectively to private persons, or the state, or to any other public authorities, or to social or co-operative organizations." Yet, according to a 2012 OCHA report, almost 1,100 Palestinians had their homes destroyed by Israeli forces in 2011. (Half of those displaced individuals were children.) The Israeli government also destroyed 622 structures owned by Palestinians, including 170 animal shelters, two classrooms, and two mosques.

In East Jerusalem today there are at least 93,100 residents who live at risk of having their homes demolished because they were built without a permit. Americans may wonder why Palestinians do not simply apply for and obtain the necessary permits so that demolition of their homes cannot be threatened. The OCHA report explains:

> According to Israeli authorities, demolitions are carried out because structures lack the required building permits. In reality, it is almost impossible for Palestinians to obtain permits. The zoning and planning regime enforced by Israel in Area C and East Jerusalem restricts Palestinian growth and development, while providing preferential treatment for unlawful Israeli settlements.[123]

Home demolition can be a form of collective punishment, as the following example from Amnesty International shows.

> The al-Najmah family, whose son Shadi participated in a shooting attack in Netanya on 9 March 2002, in which two Israeli civilians were killed and 50 wounded, was punished for the act committed by their son. The family house in al-'Ayn refugee camp in Nablus was destroyed on 22 October 2002 at 2.30 am. Shadi's parents and siblings, including a married brother with his wife and their child, lived in the house. The powerful explosive charge used by the Israeli soldiers to blow up the al-Najmah family house also destroyed six other nearby houses in which nine families lived. The 61 inhabitants of these houses were left homeless as a result. One of the destroyed houses belonged to Maryam Sheikh. She told Amnesty International: "This was our home, for me, my three sons and my daughters-in-law and their children, 27 of us in all. One of my sons raised birds for a living; all the birds were killed when the army blew up the houses; he had 4,000 shekels worth of birds at the time. The army gave us no time to take out anything; just a few minutes to gather the children and get out of the house." The following day

the Israeli army issued a statement announcing that it had destroyed the al-Najmah house, but making no mention of the fact that six neighbouring houses were also destroyed when the soldiers blew up the al-Najmah house.[124]

Americans may find it hard to imagine such an act of collective punishment, but it does regularly take place. What would it be like to learn that one of your neighbor's sons is guilty of a despicable crime and then learn that your house is going to be destroyed as punishment?

Life in the West Bank is difficult. In his book *Palestine Inside Out*, Saree Makdisi provides a summary of what it is like for Palestinians to live there:

> Although the conflict between Israelis and Palestinians is usually given international media coverage only during episodes of large-scale physical violence, such violence is still the exception rather than the rule.... The overwhelming majority of the daily encounters between Israel and the Palestinians occur in those everyday places where Israeli policy becomes Palestinian reality....
>
> In many cases, a Palestinian cannot work, travel, study, tend crops, transport goods, dig for water, start a business, obtain medical care—or even visit relatives in the next town—without obtaining the appropriate permission from the Israeli authorities. And, beyond that, her life is subject to an ever-changing and unpredictable web of curfews, checkpoints, roadblocks, ditches, walls, fences, closures, whose very randomness helps keep Palestinians off-balance.[125]

## LIFE IN GAZA

Israeli politicians point with pride to their unilateral withdrawal from the Gaza Strip in 2005, and news media in the United States are quick to report when rockets are fired from Gaza into Israel. It appears that the people of Gaza received the freedom they so desired only to respond by continuing to kill Israelis. Israel has had no choice but to defend itself against such unwarranted aggression.

Certainly the situation looks bad. Since 2005 the Israeli Defense Force

## The Present Situation

has found it necessary to intervene militarily in Gaza on three occasions. Operation Cast Lead, conducted during a three-week period in December 2008 and January 2009, resulted in at least 1,100 Palestinian and thirteen Israeli (three civilian) deaths. In November 2012, Operation Pillar of Defense was launched. During its eight-day duration, more than one hundred Palestinian and thirteen Israelis (four civilians) died. Operation Protective Edge was carried out in July and August of 2014. This fifty-day operation resulted in 2,100 Palestinians being killed and seventy-one Israelis (five civilians) dying.[126]

Questions immediately arise. Why didn't the people in Gaza eagerly embrace the freedom Israel granted them? In 2014, why did the leaders in Gaza continue to fight when so many of their own people were being killed? The answers seem obvious. Palestinians have an undying hatred for Israel, and their leaders have a callous disregard for human life. But is that the whole story? An investigation is once again called for.

Israel's unilateral withdrawal from the Gaza Strip was not as generous as it has been made out to be. Ben White in *Israeli Apartheid* provides additional information that needs to be considered.

> In fact, Israel retained control over the Strip's borders, air space and territorial waters, the population registry, export and import abilities, and crossings. Moreover, the Israeli military continued to routinely conduct ground raids inside the Strip, using the airforce for assassinations, spying missions, and collective punishment.[127]

In June of 2012 the OCHA produced a fact sheet titled "Five Years of Blockade: The Humanitarian Situation in the Gaza Strip." It stated that fuel and electricity shortages since the withdrawal resulted in outages that could last up to twelve hours a day. Water was also in short supply. Over 90 percent of the water from the Gaza aquifer was unsafe for human consumption if not treated. A number equal to 34 percent of Gaza's workforce (including half of its youth) was unemployed. Another depressing statistic revealed that 35 percent of Gaza's farmland and 85 percent of its fishing waters were totally or partially inaccessible due to Israeli imposed restrictions.[128] The OCHA reported in July 2013 that Israel had tightened restrictions on Palestinian access to the sea. Fishermen were allowed access to less than one third of the fishing area allocated under the Oslo Accords. In the first half of 2007, an average of thirty-eight truckloads of goods left Gaza per day, but in the first half of 2013 less than one truckload of goods exited Gaza.[129]

Just four months prior to Operation Protective Edge, the OCHA issued another fact sheet reporting that 30 percent of households in Gaza received running water once every four days for only six to eight hours. Furthermore, over 90 million liters of partially treated sewage were dumped in the Mediterranean Sea each day.[130] Israel had withdrawn from Gaza, but it continued to make life there unbearable.

The conflict in Gaza must not be divorced from its historical context. It did not come about overnight. As the UN Secretary-General Ban Ki-moon observed, "Yet we must not lose sight of the root causes of the recent hostilities: a restrictive occupation that has lasted almost half a century, the continued denial of Palestinian rights and the lack of tangible progress in peace negotiations."[131]

Miko Peled is an Israeli citizen and a veteran of the Israeli Defense Force. He is also the son of Matti Peled, a respected Israeli general in the 1967 war. Peled provides an example of what he learned after talking to soldiers who had helped maintain Israel's control over Gaza's borders:

> One of the guys was an officer in Israel's naval special forces, a captain in the revered Naval Commandos. He told us once how he and his unit would patrol the Gaza coast aboard their naval warships. They would come upon Gazan fishing boats and from time to time they would single out a particular boat, order the fishermen to jump into the water and blow up the boat. Then under gunpoint, they told the fishermen to count from one to a hundred and then when they were done to start over again. They would make them count over and over again until one by one the fishermen could no longer tread water, and they drowned.
>
> The young Israeli officer said this was done, as he put it, "to set an example, and teach the Arabs who was boss." I thought I was going to throw up when I heard this, but over the years I heard many similar stories from Israeli soldiers.[132]

Gaza is free in name only. It is more accurately described as the world's largest open-air prison. Michael Lerner questions Israel's portrayal of the situation:

> Imagine if some people invaded your home, then proclaimed they were leaving but instead stayed outside and prevented you from going in and out most of the time. Well, you might be happy that they were no longer inside, but you'd hardly celebrate this as "freedom." Nor would you understand how the invader could possibly claim credit for having "given" you back your home.[133]

## Terrorism, Hamas, and Islam

Americans hear regularly about the terrorism perpetrated by groups like Hamas and Islamic Jihad.[134] What can be said in defense of suicide bombers blowing up pizzerias and buses? How can the tunnels that terrorists have built from Gaza into Israel be excused? What justification can there be for launching rockets into the Israeli city of Sderot? Needless to say, those are evil acts that should be denounced. But they also need to be explained. Why *have* some factions among the Palestinian people resorted to suicide bombings that kill Israeli civilians? Why were members of Hamas elected to parliament in the Gaza Strip? What role does radical Islam play in the conflict between the Palestinians and the Israelis?

First, it must be remembered that not all Palestinians are Muslims or terrorists. To accuse every man, woman, and child who lives in the West Bank or the Gaza Strip of being an adherent of radical Islam is a blatant example of ethnic stereotyping.

Second, the use of terrorism must be placed in historical perspective. Americans often assume that only the Palestinians are guilty of terrorism, but it was Jewish militias who began to set off bombs in civilian settings.[135] According to Israeli historian Benny Morris, from "the end of 1937 until the middle of 1939, in less than two years, the terrorist activities of the Irgun and Lehi [aka the Stern Gang] claimed 232 victims with another 370 wounded—men, women and children."[136] Two former prime ministers of Israel, Menachem Begin and Yitzhak Shamir, were leaders of those Jewish terrorist groups.

Third, terrorism is often a product of desperation. Since the passing of UN Resolution 194 in 1948, the world has been promising the Palestinians that they would have the right to return to their homes. Since 1967, the Palestinians in the West Bank have been under the control of the Israelis. Even though Israeli settlements violate international law, Israel continues to build them. The United States has done virtually nothing over the last forty-five years to stop the construction of those illegal settlements.[137] As former US Secretary of State Condoleezza Rice said, "The prolonged experience of deprivation and humiliation can radicalize even normal people."[138]

Fourth, the media do not generally report on nonviolent acts of protest that regularly take place in the West Bank. In the town of Bil'in, there are demonstrations every Friday against the occupation. How often do Americans read about those nonviolent marches? Has the media in the United States skewed the picture of Palestinians and left the impression that they are all terrorists?

In 2006 the Palestinians in the Gaza Strip voted for members of Hamas and elected them the majority party in their parliament. Hamas is a militant Islamic party that the United States refuses to recognize because it is a "terrorist organization." Americans can easily interpret that election as a sign that the Palestinians in Gaza do not want to live in peace with Israel, but other factors should be taken into consideration. First, the election of Hamas was a protest against the corruption of the leaders of the ruling Fatah party. Second, it was a rejection of Israel's refusal to work with moderate Palestinians in finding solutions to the Palestinian-Israeli conflict. Third, the choice of Hamas sent a message to the United States that its efforts to bring peace to the land have failed. Fourth, Hamas was elected because of its humanitarian work in providing for the poor among the Palestinians.

An additional issue should also be faced in evaluating Hamas. The United States proclaims that it supports the spread of democracy, but its rejection of the democratically elected Hamas government in Gaza reveals America's hypocrisy. The United States will actually recognize only democratically elected governments that agree with its foreign policy.[139]

So what about the role of radical Islam? The impression is often given through the media that radical Islam, also known as Islamism, is mainly responsible for the conflict in Israel and Palestine. Colin Chapman, former lecturer in Islamic studies at the Near East School of Theology in Beirut, warns against making such quick and broad generalizations:

> Islamism in the Palestinian context has developed *gradually* over the years.
>
> This development has to be understood in the context of the occupation of the West Bank, Gaza and Lebanon. I would dare to suggest that if Israel had complied with the famous UN Resolution 242 in 1967, Hamas might never have come into existence. And if Israel had not invaded Lebanon in 1982, there might be no Hizbullah today.[140]

What do Palestinian Christians say about the role of Islam in the Palestinian-Israeli conflict? Munther Isaac is the vice academic dean at Bethlehem Bible College. He understands the economic, social, and religious pressure that Christians in the West Bank and Gaza face, and he knows why many Christians have chosen to leave their homeland. Isaac comments:

> This is a serious issue for Palestinian Christians. We are not saying that radical Islam is not a threat. We are not denying that there are some struggles that we face as a minority. We are not denying that there are some incidences in which Christians were attacked by radical Muslims…
>
> What we are saying, is that for us, the real issue and the core of our struggles is the Israeli occupation. The occupation is real. It has been our reality for the last 45 years. It is the main reason why Palestinian Christians are leaving. Every Palestinian Christian leader and every major Christian movement, Orthodox, Catholics, and Protestants alike, have stressed this.[141]

Alex Awad speaks from his experience as a pastor, Bible college teacher, and former president of the Council of Local Evangelical Churches in the Holy Land:

I have lived most of my life as a member of a small Christian community within a larger Islamic population. The Church that I now pastor in East Jerusalem is located in a predominantly Muslim neighborhood. I know from first-hand experience and from daily contacts with Muslims that most Muslims do not hate Christians. Moreover, most Muslims have nothing to do with terrorism.[142]

The point must again be made that these observations do not excuse terrorism. All acts of terrorism should be denounced. But those acts also need to be explained. There is more to the situation than meets the American eye.

## Israeli and American Jewish Perspectives

The picture of modern Israel portrayed in this chapter is so different from the one that Americans usually see that it is natural to question whether it can be trusted. But this understanding of Israel comes not just from the United Nations or from enemies of Israel. Leaders in Israel and Jews in America today also question the path that Israel is pursuing.

Shlomo Ben-Ami, former Israeli foreign minister, questions what Israel has been doing in the West Bank since 1967:

> Through what was, and continues to be, the most absurd march of folly that the State of Israel has ever embarked on—the creation of a dense map of settlements throughout the territories that narrowed the living space of the Palestinian people—Israel destroyed beyond repair the faith of its Palestinian partners in the peace process.[143]

Avraham Burg, former speaker of the Israeli Knesset, reflects on the way Israel has treated the Palestinians:

> The Shoah [Holocaust] sensitized governments and organizations to anti-Semitism and other hate crimes. Even the Catholic Church's dogmatic change of attitude toward Jews and human rights every-

where happened because of the Shoah. In contrast, we have never done anything similar for the Palestinian refugees and their descendants. We did not fulfill what we demanded of others. Therefore we must stand on the tallest mountain and declare clearly and loudly: we know that solving the Shoah refugee problem directly and indirectly caused the Palestinian refugee problem....

What is most important is the recognition of the suffering and assuming of responsibility, even partial and belated, for the distress of the Palestinian refugees. Only with recognition and sharing will it be possible to rebuild the relations between the two great refugee cultures that came to the same piece of land to build anew from the ruins.[144]

Henry Siegman, who is president of the US/Middle East Project and was the head of the American Jewish Congress from 1978 to 1994, writes:

The Middle East peace process may well be the most spectacular deception in modern diplomatic history. Since the failed Camp David summit of 2000, and actually well before it, Israel's interest in a peace process—other than for the purpose of obtaining Palestinian and international acceptance of the status quo—has been a fiction that has served primarily to provide cover for its systematic confiscation of Palestinian land.[145]

Mark Braverman is an American Jew with strong ties to modern Israel. Five generations of his family have lived in the land. In 1965, when he was seventeen years old, he spent a year working on a kibbutz in Israel. He was proud of Israel and loved Israel. In 2006 he returned and grieved over what he saw in the nation he loved:

Over the years, living for a time in Israel and visiting frequently, I became increasingly concerned about Israel's treatment of the Palestinians and about its illegal settlement activity. Still, I held to the Zionist narrative: Israel's militarism and expansionism were the price of security. Then I went to the West Bank. I saw the separation wall and knew it was not for defense. I saw the damage inflicted by the checkpoints on Palestinian life and on the souls and psyches of my Jewish cousins in uniform. I saw the Jewish-only settlements and the restricted roads. I witnessed the vicious acts of ideological Jewish settlers. I learned that the events of 1948, what I had been taught to call the War of Liberation, were for Palestinians the Nakba. As my defenses against the recognition of Israel's crimes crumbled, my fear for my own people grew. It grew in proportion to my horror, anger and sadness over the injustice that was being perpetrated in my name.[146]

An honest investigation into the discrimination that Palestinian citizens of Israel face and the oppression that Palestinians in the occupied territories must endure inevitably leads to an unavoidable question: Why do Americans in general and evangelical Christians in particular give their unqualified support to modern Israel?

The answer lies not so much in our knowledge of the past and the present as in our understanding and application of the Bible's teaching. So now we turn to examine the belief system that has given rise to unquestioning support for Israel.

# Part Two
# Bible and Theology

*Chapter Four*
# The Old Testament and Modern Israel

*Blessed are those who act justly,
who always do what is right.*

PSALM 106:3

OVER BREAKFAST A FRIEND AND I were discussing the Middle East and the ongoing difficulties in establishing peace between the Palestinians and Israelis. We talked about the history of the conflict, the current stalemate between the two sides, and the role of the United States. Finally my friend leaned forward and said, "But what about Genesis 12:3? God says to Israel that 'I will bless those who bless you, and whoever curses you I will curse.' Isn't that everything a Christian needs to know? Obviously God wants us to be on Israel's side!"

With that statement my friend summarized the majority evangelical position in America today. Christians whose allegiance is foremost to God sincerely see themselves as mandated to support modern Israel. But is unequivocal support for Israel truly required—or even warranted—by the teachings of the Bible?

## THE KEY VERSE

Genesis 12:3 is the most frequently quoted Bible verse in support of the theological perspective known as Christian Zionism. At its most fundamental level Christian Zionism is the belief that God expects Christians to provide strong support for the modern nation of Israel. Christian Zionism is a broad and diverse movement, but its most vocal proponents teach that Genesis 12:3 applies to modern Israel in the same way it applied to ancient Israel.[147]

According to Christian Zionism, blessing the modern nation of Israel is God's stated and unambiguous will for us. Furthermore, seeking the good of Israel bestows God's favor upon the nations that do so. In other words, blessing Israel is politically wise. If the United States or any nation wants to receive God's protection and provision, then it must strive to support and encourage Israel through its foreign policy. To do otherwise would be to bring God's curse upon one's own nation.[148] Pastor John Hagee, one of Christian Zionism's strongest advocates, states, "It is an undeniable fact that the man or the nation that has blessed Israel has been blessed of God, and to the man or the nation that cursed Israel the judgment of God came in spades."[149]

This widely publicized and popular understanding of Genesis 12:3 seems to be the teaching of God's Word, but it needs to be studied carefully before being immediately embraced. Even though Christian Zionism is commonly taught in books, preached in sermons, and promoted on television, it needs to be examined to see if it truly reflects the teaching of God's Word. Failing to understand Genesis 12:3 properly could lead to harmful consequences to the people of the Middle East, to our own country, and to the glory of our God. If we find that this key verse does apply to modern Israel in the same way it applied to ancient Israel, what are the implications? Is political, economic, and military support for modern Israel the end of the matter, or could there be more that needs to be taken into consideration?

## Old Testament Law

The first question that needs to be asked when embarking on further study is "What about teaching found in other parts of the Old Testament?" If Genesis 12:3 gives authoritative instructions on how Israel is to be treated today, doesn't it follow that instructions found in other parts of the Old Testament regarding Israel's treatment of other people should be obeyed as well?

God gave laws to ancient Israel through Moses in order to instruct the people in how they were to live in the land God had given to them. Those laws include commandments about how the Israelites were to treat foreigners living in their midst:

Do not mistreat or oppress a foreigner, for you were foreigners in Egypt. (Exodus 22:21)

Do not oppress a foreigner; you yourselves know how it feels to be foreigners, because you were foreigners in Egypt. (Exodus 23:9)

When a foreigner resides among you in your land, do not mistreat them. The foreigner residing among you must be treated as your native-born. Love them as yourself, for you were foreigners in Egypt. I am the LORD your God. (Leviticus 19:33–34)

You are to have the same law for the foreigner and the native-born. I am the LORD your God. (Leviticus 24:22)

The community is to have the same rules for you and for the foreigner residing among you; this is a lasting ordinance for the generations to come. You and the foreigner shall be the same before the LORD: The same laws and regulations will apply both to you and to the foreigner residing among you. (Numbers 15:15–16)

Hear the disputes between your people and judge fairly, whether the case is between two Israelites or between an Israelite and a foreigner residing among you. (Deuteronomy 1:16)

[God] defends the cause of the fatherless and the widow, and loves the foreigner residing among you, giving them food and clothing. And you are to love those who are foreigners, for you yourselves were foreigners in Egypt. (Deuteronomy 10:18–19)

Do not deprive the foreigner or the fatherless of justice, or take the cloak of the widow as a pledge. Remember that you were slaves in Egypt and the LORD your God redeemed you from there. That is why I command you to do this. (Deuteronomy 24:17–18)

The commandments found in Exodus through Numbers speak powerfully about how the Israelites were to treat those who were not members of their nation. God commanded the Israelites not to oppress foreigners or mistreat them. Foreigners were to be treated in the same way that native-born Israelites were treated. Lawsuits between them were to be decided on the basis of justice, not ethnic background. And even more was expected: foreigners were to be loved by the Israelites.

If Christian Zionists insist that Genesis 12:3 applies to modern Israel in the same way that it did to ancient Israel, it follows that the Old Testament teaching about foreigners should be obeyed as well. The government of modern Israel should make every effort to be sure that Arabs who are Israeli citizens are granted the same privileges Jewish citizens receive. Palestinians living in the West Bank and in Gaza should be treated with justice. Jews and Arabs in the West Bank should be subject to the same set of laws. Water resources should be equally available to all. Palestinians should be allowed to drive on the same roads in the West Bank that Israeli settlers use. The Israeli courts should make sure that Palestinians in East Jerusalem are granted building permits and that due process is followed before Arab homes are destroyed.

It is sad that modern Israel does not practice justice for those they consider to be foreigners in their land. But even more tragic is the way the Old Testament laws about foreigners are ignored by Christian Zionists. They gladly declare their belief in the inspiration and authority of the Bible, but they pick and choose which verses of the Old Testament to emphasize. They are quick to quote Genesis 12:3 as a proof text on how the United States should deal with modern Israel, but they ignore the strong ethical instructions found in Exodus through Numbers that deal with the way that Israel should treat foreigners. Why do Christian Zionists not urge Israeli leaders to stop the injustices they are inflicting on the Palestinians?

## OLD TESTAMENT PROPHETS

A second line of inquiry also needs to be explored. How did God bless Israel in the Old Testament? The unspoken assumption behind Christian Zionism is that blessing Israel today means agreeing with the Israeli government's policies and supporting whatever decisions the nation's leaders make. But is that the way that God blessed ancient Israel?

## The Old Testament and Modern Israel

In the Old Testament God blessed Israel by sending his prophets to the nation to warn them of judgment and call them to repentance. Unfortunately most Christians neglect to read the prophets for themselves. It is far easier to accept someone else's conclusions about Bible prophecy—particularly if a prophecy teacher provides captivating and seemingly authoritative glimpses into what God is doing in the world today and what he will do in the near future. Understanding the writings of the prophets does require more work than reading the narratives contained in books such as Genesis or Joshua, but even a quick reading of the prophets reveals that they were not hesitant to criticize Old Testament Israel and Judah for those nations' violation of God's standards.

Around the middle of the eighth century BC, God sent the prophet Amos from the southern kingdom of Judah to the northern kingdom of Israel to call that kingdom to repentance. Amos approached ancient Israel in a way that is the opposite of the approach Christian Zionism takes. Instead of assuring the Israelites that God would unconditionally bless them, Amos stressed the nation's obligation to obey God. Precisely *because* Israel was chosen by God, the nation had a greater responsibility to repent of its sins and conform to God's standards.

> Hear this word, people of Israel, the word the LORD has spoken against you—against the whole family I brought up out of Egypt:
> "You only have I chosen
> of all the families of the earth;
> therefore I will punish you
> for all your sins."
> AMOS 3:1–2

Through his prophet, God reinforced the message of the Old Testament law about the importance of justice. If Israel failed to act justly, then God's judgment would come upon the nation.

> Seek good, not evil,
> that you may live.
> Then the LORD God Almighty will be with you,

just as you say he is.
Hate evil, love good;
>maintain justice in the courts.
Perhaps the LORD God Almighty will have mercy
>on the remnant of Joseph.
AMOS 5:14–15

Amos 5:24 summarized God's message to ancient Israel with a stirring and unforgettable image: "But let justice roll on like a river, righteousness like a never-failing stream!"

Old Testament history records that the northern kingdom of Israel refused to listen to the message of the prophets. The nation fell to the Assyrians in 722 BC. Then, in the late eighth century BC, God sent Micah to call the people in the southern kingdom of Judah to repentance:

Then I said,
"Listen, you leaders of Jacob,
>you rulers of Israel.
Should you not embrace justice,
>you who hate good and love evil;
who tear the skin from my people
>and the flesh from their bones;
who eat my people's flesh,
>strip off their skin
>and break their bones in pieces;
who chop them up like meat for the pan,
>like flesh for the pot?"
MICAH 3:1–3

Micah did not just deal with generalities. He listed specific acts that the leaders of the nation were permitting and practicing.

Am I still to forget your ill-gotten treasures, you wicked house,
>and the short ephah, which is accursed?
Shall I acquit someone with dishonest scales,

with a bag of false weights?
MICAH 6:10–11

The prophet Isaiah was a contemporary of Micah's. He too warned the kingdom of Judah about their sins and how God would bring judgment if the leaders did not repent.

> Woe to those who make unjust laws,
> > to those who issue oppressive decrees,
> to deprive the poor of their rights
> > and withhold justice from the oppressed of my people,
> making widows their prey
> > and robbing the fatherless.
> ISAIAH 10:1–2

Like the northern kingdom of Israel, Judah did not take Micah's or Isaiah's messages to heart. As a result, God's judgment came. The Babylonian army under Nebuchadnezzar conquered and destroyed Jerusalem in 586 BC.

At the end of the sixth century BC, God sent another prophet. Zechariah spoke to the people of Judah whom God had mercifully allowed to return from their exile in Babylon.

> And the word of the LORD came again to Zechariah: "This is what the LORD Almighty said: 'Administer true justice; show mercy and compassion to one another. Do not oppress the widow or the fatherless, the foreigner or the poor. Do not plot evil against each other.'" (Zechariah 7:8–10)

Around 480 BC, God again sent a prophet to his people. Malachi's message was the same as that delivered in the Mosaic law and through the previous prophets:

You have wearied the LORD with your words.

"How have we wearied him?" you ask.

By saying, "All who do evil are good in the eyes of the LORD, and he is pleased with them" or "Where is the God of justice?"...

"So I will come to put you on trial. I will be quick to testify against sorcerers, adulterers and perjurers, against those who defraud laborers of their wages, who oppress the widows and the fatherless, and deprive the foreigners among you of justice, but do not fear me," says the LORD Almighty. (Malachi 2:17, 3:5)

God had a consistent message for his people. From the time of Moses to the period in which Malachi lived, God called upon them to practice justice.

## GOD'S MESSAGE TO MODERN ISRAEL

The Old Testament law and prophets place an obligation upon Christians today who believe that Old Testament teaching should be applied to modern Israel in the same way it applied to ancient Israel. If we are to bless Israel in the same way that the prophets did—that God himself did—we should challenge the policies of modern Israel that discriminate against Palestinians. The Old Testament law and prophets issue a demand for repentance. "Let justice roll on like a river, righteousness like a never-failing stream!"

Being true to the message of the Bible requires more than simply quoting Genesis 12:3. Relying on that one verse alone to guide our beliefs and policies leads to serious distortion of the Bible's teaching and to simplistic support for the policies of a modern nation that is sometimes far from just. In *Allies for Armageddon,* Victoria Clark observes:

> This single line of Genesis is the vital insurance policy that goes as far towards explaining the appeal of Christian Zionism as any thrillingly apocalyptic narrative or Rapture get-out clause. On the strength of that endlessly reiterated one-line promise to Abraham, millions of Americans have come to believe that if they "bless" Israel morally, financially and politically, God will reward them by favouring America. "Blessing" Israel for America's sake has been

motivating Christian Zionists to combat anti-Semitism, donate to Jewish charities, and invest in and visit Israel. But it has also involved many in opposing any peace process, in supporting the continued building of Jewish settlements in the West Bank, in funding those internationally outlawed settlements and in backing an extreme right-wing Israeli plan to "transfer" the Palestinians to neighbouring Arab states.[150]

Genesis 12:3 should not be the only part of the Bible that shapes Christians' views about Israel today. The message of the Old Testament law and prophets must be factored in. God's blessing of Israel was never unequivocal. Neither should ours be.

For many Christians this chapter will be sufficient to compel them to reconsider the unqualified support they have previously given to Israel. They might want to proceed immediately to chapter 9. But to be faithful to the total teaching of God's Word, another step must be taken. We need to go a step further and consider the New Testament's treatment of the Old Testament. Particular attention must be paid to its understanding of the promise that God made to Abraham and his descendants in Genesis 12:3.

*Chapter Five*
# The Old Testament Fulfilled

✡

*These are a shadow of the things that were to come;
the reality, however, is found in Christ.*

Colossians 2:16

I THOUGHT IT WOULD JUST BE A SIMPLE BIBLE STUDY. In order to appreciate how God fulfilled his promise to bring his Messiah to Israel, I planned to read through the four Gospels. Whenever Matthew, Mark, Luke, or John indicated that an Old Testament prophecy had been fulfilled in Jesus, I would read the entire prophecy for myself. Reading the prediction in its original setting and then marveling at how Jesus fulfilled it in the New Testament could not help but be an inspiring and worshipful experience.

## The Problem

But that's not how it turned out. The more I compared the Old Testament prophecies to their fulfillment described by the Gospel writers, the more puzzling my simple Bible study became. I still maintained my conviction about the inspiration and trustworthiness of the Bible, but the problem kept getting bigger and more confusing.

The first major stumbling block came when I read Matthew's account of Joseph, Mary, and Jesus in Egypt.

> So he got up, took the child and his mother during the night and left for Egypt, where he stayed until the death of Herod. And so

was fulfilled what the Lord had said through the prophet: "Out of Egypt I called my son." (Matthew 2:15–16)

Matthew's account *seems* so straightforward. Joseph took Mary and Jesus to Egypt in order to escape from Herod's plot to kill Jesus. After Joseph heard the news that Herod had died, he took his wife and child back to their homeland. Matthew says it was just what the prophet Hosea had predicted: "Out of Egypt I called my son."

But I quickly discovered a problem. In Hosea 11:1, the prophet was not making a prediction. Instead, he was remembering the exodus from Egypt under Moses's leadership.

> When Israel was a child, I loved him,
>     and out of Egypt I called my son.
> But the more they were called,
>     the more they went away from me.
> They sacrificed to the Baals
>     and they burned incense to images.
> HOSEA 11:1–2

Hosea was not making a prediction about what God would do with his Messiah centuries later. In fact, he was not making a prediction at all! Hosea was reminding the people of his day what God had done centuries before and how Israel had sunk into idolatry after they entered the Promised Land. I wondered how Matthew could take that historical recollection and turn it into a prediction for the future. Matthew *seemed* to be unquestionably wrong.

The puzzle only grew deeper the more I studied the Gospels. John's gospel records what the soldiers did with Jesus's clothes when they crucified him:

> When the soldiers crucified Jesus, they took his clothes, dividing them into four shares, one for each of them, with the undergarment remaining. This garment was seamless, woven in one piece from top to bottom.

## The Old Testament Fulfilled

"Let's not tear it," they said to one another. "Let's decide by lot who will get it."

This happened that the scripture might be fulfilled that said,

> "They divided my clothes among them
> and cast lots for my garment."

So this is what the soldiers did.

JOHN 19:23–24

Once again the prediction *seems* straightforward. The Messiah's clothes were to be divided among his enemies, and the recipients of his clothes would be determined by casting lots. John makes it appear that God had predicted the details of what would happen when Jesus was crucified.

But when I turned to Psalm 22, the origin of the words John quoted, my comparison of the Gospels and the Old Testament hit another roadblock. I could find no indication in Psalm 22 that David was making a prediction about God's chosen Messiah. Instead, David seems to be describing nothing more than his own experience:

> Dogs surround me,
> a pack of villains encircles me;
> they pierce my hands and my feet.
> All my bones are on display;
> people stare and gloat over me.
> They divide my clothes among them
> and cast lots for my garment.
> But you, LORD, do not be far from me.
> You are my strength; come quickly to help me.
> Deliver me from the sword,
> my precious life from the power of the dogs.

PSALM 22:16–20

Again I wondered: How could John take a descriptive statement about David's personal experience and turn it into a prediction of what would happen centuries later to Jesus?

John also describes how the soldiers did not need to break Jesus's legs when he was hanging on the cross because he was already dead. John seems once again to see a precise fulfillment of the Old Testament.

> These things happened so that the scripture would be fulfilled: "Not one of his bones will be broken." (John 19:36)

Three different Old Testament verses can be cited as the source of the prediction that John says was fulfilled through the soldiers' inaction: Exodus 12:46, Numbers 9:12, and Psalm 34:20. Even a quick examination of those passages reveals a problem once more.

> The LORD said to Moses and Aaron, "These are the regulations for the Passover meal:
> "No foreigner may eat it. Any slave you have bought may eat it after you have circumcised him, but a temporary resident or a hired worker may not eat it.
> "It must be eaten inside the house; take none of the meat outside the house. Do not break any of the bones. The whole community of Israel must celebrate it." (Exodus 12:43–46)

> Then the LORD said to Moses, "Tell the Israelites: 'When any of you or your descendants are unclean because of a dead body or are away on a journey, they are still to celebrate the LORD's Passover, but they are to do it on the fourteenth day of the second month at twilight. They are to eat the lamb, together with unleavened bread and bitter herbs. They must not leave any of it till morning or break any of its bones. When they celebrate the Passover, they must follow all the regulations.'" (Numbers 9:9–12)

> The righteous person may have many troubles,
>   but the LORD delivers him from them all;
> he protects all his bones,
>   not one of them will be broken.
> PSALM 34:19–20

# The Old Testament Fulfilled

The passages in Exodus and Numbers were not predictions waiting to be fulfilled; they were instructions about how the Passover lamb was to be handled. Why does John turn them into predictions? With Psalm 34, John seems to be making the same "mistake" that he makes in his treatment of Psalm 22. Why does John take a generic statement about "the righteous person" and say it was a prediction about Jesus?

The gospel of Luke provided me with more unsettling questions. Luke records what Jesus said to the two disciples who were walking with him on the road to Emmaus after his resurrection. Then he provides a comment that summarizes the conclusion of their conversation:

> And He said to them, "O foolish men and slow of heart to believe in all that the prophets have spoken! Was it not necessary for the Christ to suffer these things and to enter into His glory?" Then beginning with Moses and with all the prophets, He explained to them the things concerning Himself in all the Scriptures. (Luke 24:25–27, NASB)

What did Jesus mean when he mentioned "the things concerning himself in all the Scriptures"? I wondered how "all the Scriptures" could be thought of as saying something about Jesus. There may have been some specific predictions in the Old Testament about God's Messiah, but it seems like Luke is exaggerating when he writes that "all the Scriptures" were about Jesus!

Throughout this journey I continued to believe in the inspiration and total trustworthiness of the Bible, but I was confused. What had started off as a simple Bible study ended not in inspiration but in bewilderment. To put it frankly, the writers of the Gospels seemed to be cheating. Out of their devotion to Jesus, they seemed to have written books to draw other people to him by twisting Old Testament passages to make their case more convincing. At least, that is the way that it *seems*!

But my ongoing belief in the inerrancy of the Bible made me suspect that something was missing in my analysis. I wondered if it was possible that I had missed something deeper and far more profound at work in the New Testament's approach to the Old Testament. The journey was not over. I still had a lot to learn.

## Jesus and the Old Testament

In the Sermon on the Mount, Jesus addressed an important first-century issue concerning the Law of Moses. He said, "Do not think that I have come to abolish the Law or the Prophets; I have not come to abolish them but to fulfill them" (Matthew 5:17).

What did Jesus mean when he said that he came to "fulfill" the Old Testament Law? That statement has been understood in various ways. Some interpreters suggest that Jesus was teaching that he would explain the true meaning of the Old Testament commandments or that he would expand on the full meaning of the laws given by Moses. But perhaps Jesus was teaching that the laws themselves had some kind of predictive message that he had come to fulfill.

REST. Consider what else Jesus said about the Old Testament. Matthew 11 concludes with his well-known statement of comfort:

> Come to me, all you who are weary and burdened, and I will give you rest. Take my yoke upon you and learn from me, for I am gentle and humble in heart, and you will find rest for your souls. For my yoke is easy and my burden is light. (Matthew 11:28–30)

Jesus promised "rest" to his disciples. Modern minds immediately think of rest in therapeutic terms. To rest means to relax and be refreshed. But in the Old Testament rest was not about therapy but about theology.

The Old Testament frequently connected rest to the Sabbath day, on which God himself had rested:

> By the seventh day God had finished the work he had been doing; so on the seventh day he rested from all his work. Then God blessed the seventh day and made it holy, because on it he rested from all the work of creating that he had done. (Genesis 2:2–3)

In the Ten Commandments, God told the Israelites that they were to follow his example. The word *Sabbath* comes from the Hebrew term meaning rest, and the Sabbath day was intended to be a day of rest for the Israelites.

> Remember the Sabbath day by keeping it holy. Six days you shall labor and do all your work, but the seventh day is a sabbath to the LORD your God. On it you shall not do any work, neither you, nor your son or daughter, nor your male or female servant, nor your animals, nor any foreigner residing in your towns. For in six days the LORD made the heavens and the earth, the sea, and all that is in them, but he rested on the seventh day. Therefore the LORD blessed the Sabbath day and made it holy. (Exodus 20:8–11)

In other Old Testament passages that gave instructions for the Sabbath, the importance of rest was likewise emphasized:

> Six days you shall labor, but on the seventh day you shall rest; even during the plowing season and harvest you must rest. (Exodus 34:21)

Could it be that Jesus had such Old Testament passages in mind when he told his disciples that he would give them "rest" in the last three verses of Matthew? And if he did, what are the implications?

That understanding of Jesus's promise finds confirmation in the opening verses of the following chapter. The uninspired and unfortunate chapter division between Matthew 11 and 12 separates two parts of Jesus's teaching that belong together. Matthew 11:28–30 is the beginning of a teaching portion that explains Jesus' relationship to the Sabbath day. In Matthew 11 Jesus explains that he provides the rest that the Old Testament Sabbath promised. Matthew 12:1–8 then goes on to underline that teaching by recording examples of Jesus's activities on the Sabbath. Taken as a whole, Matthew 11:28–12:8 presents Jesus in word and deed as fulfilling the divine intention behind the Old Testament Sabbath.

In the midst of that teaching about the Sabbath in Matthew 12, Jesus made another surprising and thought-provoking statement. He referred to himself and said, "I tell you, something greater than the temple is here" (Matthew 12:6). Jesus moved from comparing himself to the Sabbath to comparing himself to another central institution of Israel's religious life—and once more, presenting himself as the fulfillment of that institution.

TEMPLE. According to the Old Testament, the temple was the location of God's presence among his people. King Solomon dedicated the temple, and God confirmed his presence through miracle and word.

> When Solomon finished praying, fire came down from heaven and consumed the burnt offering and the sacrifices, and the glory of the LORD filled the temple. The priests could not enter the temple of the LORD because the glory of the LORD filled it. When all the Israelites saw the fire coming down and the glory of the LORD above the temple, they knelt on the pavement with their faces to the ground....
>
> "I have heard the prayer and plea you have made before me; I have consecrated this temple, which you have built, by putting my Name there forever. My eyes and my heart will always be there." (2 Chronicles 7:1–3, 1 Kings 9:3)

The temple was central to Israel's worship of God. Therefore, Jesus's declaration that he was "greater than the temple" was shocking.

The second chapter of John's gospel records the incident in which Jesus expelled the moneychangers from the temple:

> The Jews then responded to him, "What sign can you show us to prove your authority to do all this?"
>
> Jesus answered them, "Destroy this temple, and I will raise it again in three days."
>
> They replied, "It has taken forty-six years to build this temple, and you are going to raise it in three days?" But the temple he had spoken of was his body. (John 2:18–21)

Once again Jesus compared himself to the temple and indicated that he in some way surpassed or fulfilled it. This pattern—of drawing on events, institutions, and commandments in the Old Testament and then declaring himself the "fulfillment" of them—continues.

MANNA. John 6 includes one of Jesus's memorable "I am" statements. He built it directly on the Old Testament—and once more, it is not built on a predictive prophecy but on a past event.

## The Old Testament Fulfilled

I am the bread of life. Your ancestors ate the manna in the wilderness, yet they died. But here is the bread that comes down from heaven, which anyone may eat and not die. I am the living bread that came down from heaven. Whoever eats this bread will live forever. This bread is my flesh, which I will give for the life of the world. (John 6:48–51)

In this passage Jesus portrayed himself as the fulfillment of an Old Testament event (Exodus 16:13–36), but he went even further. In similar fashion to his teaching about the temple, Jesus taught his superiority to the Old Testament manna. That manna had provided Israel with physical nourishment, but Jesus claimed to provide bread that would enable his followers to "live forever." Once again Jesus took something from the Old Testament and taught that it was fulfilled in himself.

PASSOVER. Jesus had something even more surprising to teach his disciples. One of the most shocking things he ever did took place on the night before his death.

And he took bread, gave thanks and broke it, and gave it to them, saying, "This is my body given for you; do this in remembrance of me."
In the same way, after the supper he took the cup, saying, "This cup is the new covenant in my blood, which is poured out for you." (Luke 22:19–20)

Because Christians are so well acquainted with the Lord's Supper, they miss the astounding nature of what Jesus said at that meal. Jesus took a traditional Jewish meal and applied it in a new way. For over a thousand years the Jews had eaten the bread and shared a cup of wine on that special night of the year called Passover. Every year they participated in the Passover meal in order to remind themselves of how God rescued their ancestors from Egypt (Exodus 12:24–28). But Jesus offered an entirely new application of the meal. He gave his disciples the bread and said, "This is *my* body." Then he gave them the cup and said, "Do this in remembrance of *me*." In effect, Jesus taught, "Don't think about Egypt and what God did back then. From now on when you eat this meal, I want you to think about me."

Imagine a national leader in modern America saying that from now on, the Fourth of July should be a celebration of himself. "Don't think about the Declaration of Independence or the birth of our country. I'm more important than George Washington or Thomas Jefferson. From now on the Fourth of July parade should be in honor of me!"

That is what Jesus was doing at his Last Supper with his disciples. Jesus took the Passover meal and used it to call attention to himself. The way that God had rescued Israel from Egypt was extraordinary, but now something far more important was taking place. Jesus taught that he was the fulfillment of the Passover. Not only that, but he declared that the Passover had never ultimately been about deliverance from Egypt. It had been a prophecy: a shadow of Jesus who was to come.

Jesus used the Old Testament in a way that no one in his day expected. He proclaimed himself to be the fulfillment of the Mosaic law, the Sabbath, the temple, the manna, and the Passover. Jesus saw himself as the fulfillment of the entire Old Testament.

## THE GOSPELS AND THE OLD TESTAMENT

The writers of the four Gospels followed the example of their Lord and portrayed him in distinctly Old Testament terms. For example, Matthew and Luke's versions of Jesus's temptation by the devil provide a comparison between Israel's experience in the wilderness and Jesus's experience in the same locale.

> Then Jesus was led by the Spirit into the wilderness to be tempted by the devil. After fasting forty days and forty nights, he was hungry. The tempter came to him and said, "If you are the Son of God, tell these stones to become bread."
>
> Jesus answered, "It is written: 'Man shall not live on bread alone, but on every word that comes from the mouth of God.'"
>
> Then the devil took him to the holy city and had him stand on the highest point of the temple. "If you are the Son of God," he said, "throw yourself down. For it is written:
> 'He will command his angels concerning you,

and they will lift you up in their hands,
so that you will not strike your foot against a stone.'"

Jesus answered him, "It is also written: 'Do not put the Lord your God to the test.'"

Again, the devil took him to a very high mountain and showed him all the kingdoms of the world and their splendor. "All this I will give you," he said, "if you will bow down and worship me."

Jesus said to him, "Away from me, Satan! For it is written: 'Worship the Lord your God, and serve him only.'"

Then the devil left him, and angels came and attended him. (Matthew 4:1–11)

The similarities between Israel and Jesus in this story are noteworthy. Israel wandered in the wilderness for forty years (Deuteronomy 8:2); Jesus was tempted in the wilderness for forty days and forty nights. Jesus's three responses to the devil's temptations are all drawn from Deuteronomy's record of Israel's experience in the wilderness (Deuteronomy 8:3, 6:16, 6:13). What is more striking than the similarities is the difference. Israel failed to obey God during its wilderness wanderings, but Jesus did not give in to the devil's temptations. In other words, Jesus accomplished what Israel could not.

The gospel of John also portrays Jesus as similar but superior to Israel. That comparison begins in John's opening section:

The Word became flesh and made his dwelling among us. We have seen his glory, the glory of the one and only Son, who came from the Father, full of grace and truth. (John 1:14)

Based on this single verse, two parallels can be drawn between Israel and Jesus. First, Jesus is called God's Son in the same way that Israel was called God's son (Exodus 4:22–23, Jeremiah 31:9, Hosea 11:1). Second, the word the New International Version translates "dwelling" is the Greek term for "tent" or "tabernacle." That single word provides a verbal echo of the Old Testament's teaching about the tabernacle. In the Old Testament that sacred tent was the dwelling place of God's glory; in the New Testament

God dwells in Jesus. In the Old Testament the tabernacle was filled with the glory of God, and not even Moses was allowed to enter it and view God's visible glory (Exodus 40:34–35). In contrast, Jesus's disciples "have seen his glory." Jesus opened up a possibility that was not allowed in the Old Testament. God's people were no longer forbidden to encounter God's glory.

John 1:14 expands on what Jesus himself taught. Jesus was similar but superior to Israel.

## The Answer to the Problem

Jesus's use of the Old Testament answers the problem I encountered in my study of the Old Testament prophecies and their fulfillment in the four Gospels. What had appeared to be cheating on the part of Matthew, Mark, Luke, and John turned out to be something far more profound than the fulfillment of specific predictions. The writers were not distorting the Old Testament writings at all; rather, they were following Jesus's lead in seeing the Old Testament fulfilled in him.

God showed what he planned for the future in more ways than just making predictions. He also provided pictures and patterns in religious practices, buildings, events, and ceremonies. Jesus repeatedly dropped hints that those Old Testament models were not complete in themselves. Instead, they suggested something better that was yet to come.[151] God's work in human history was not haphazard but consistent. His acts on behalf of his people followed patterns that grew and expanded until they reached their ultimate expression in Jesus.

When Matthew writes that Hosea 11:1 was fulfilled in Jesus, he is building on the parallel between Israel's experience as God's son and Jesus's experience as God's Son. Just as God brought the nation of Israel out of Egypt in the exodus under Moses, so God would bring his one and only Son, Jesus, out of Egypt too.

When John writes that Psalm 22:16–18 was fulfilled at Jesus's crucifixion when the soldiers cast lots for his clothes, he bases that claim on the parallel between Jesus's experience at the cross and David's experience with his enemies. That is not a distortion of the Old Testament because Jesus was the long-awaited descendant of King David whom the Old Testament prophets had said would come and provide for God's people. It is legitimate

## The Old Testament Fulfilled

to see David's experience fulfilled in a more complete sense by his royal descendant, Jesus.

The same line of logic is evident in John's reference to none of Jesus's bones being broken at his crucifixion. The passages from Exodus and Numbers about the Passover lamb's bones are cited because Jesus was the ultimate Lamb of God (John 1:30) who made the complete and final sacrifice for sin. John can also have Psalm 34:20 in mind because Jesus was the ultimate embodiment of "the righteous person" being described in that psalm.

Bible scholars refer to this kind of fulfillment as "typological." A *type* is an Old Testament place, event, institution, office, object, or even person that serves as a foreshadowing of what God had planned for the future. The experience and institutions of ancient Israel are examples of Old Testament types.

|  | Israel | Jesus |
| --- | --- | --- |
| **Experience** | Exodus from Egypt<br>Hosea 11:1 | "Out of Egypt I called my son"<br>Matthew 2:15 |
|  | The Passover<br>Exodus 12:24-28 | The Lord's Supper<br>Luke 22:19-20 |
|  | 40 years in the wilderness<br>Deuteronomy 8:2 | 40 days & nights in the wilderness<br>Matthew 4:1-11 |
|  | Manna<br>Exodus 16:13-36 | "I am the bread of life"<br>John 6:48 |
|  | Trials of King David<br>Psalm 22:16-20 | Sufferings of the Son of David<br>John 19:23-24 |
| **Institutions** | The Law and the Prophets | "I have come to fulfill them"<br>Matthew 5:17 |
|  | Sabbath<br>Exodus 31:15 | "I will give you rest"<br>Matt. 11:28-29 |
|  | The Tabernacle<br>Exodus 25:8 | "He made his dwelling among us"<br>John 1:14 |
|  | The Temple<br>Deuteronomy 12:5 | "One greater than the Temple"<br>Matthew 12:6; John 4:20-23 |

The nation of Israel itself is a type of Christ. New Testament scholar R.T. France summarizes the New Testament's typological portrayal of Jesus this way:

> Jesus' types are drawn from a wide range of aspects of Israel seen in the Old Testament; they are not restricted to any one period or any single class. Thus he uses *persons* in the Old Testament as types of himself (David, Solomon, Elijah, Elisha, Isaiah, Jonah) or of John the Baptist (Elijah); he refers to Old Testament *institutions* as types of himself and his work (the priesthood and the covenant); he sees in the *experiences* of Israel foreshadowings of his own; he finds the *hopes* of Israel fulfilled in himself and his disciples and sees his disciples as assuming the *status* of Israel; in Israel's *deliverance* by God he sees a type of the gathering of men into his church....
>
> In all these aspects of the Old Testament people of God Jesus sees foreshadowings of himself and his work.... Thus in his coming the history of Israel has reached its decisive point. The whole of the Old Testament is gathered up in him. He himself embodies in his own person the status and destiny of Israel, and in the community of those who belong to him that status and destiny are to be fulfilled, no longer in the nation as such.[152]

That, in effect, is what Jesus says about himself on the road to Emmaus: "Then beginning with Moses and with all the prophets, He explained to them the things concerning Himself in *all the Scriptures*" (Luke 24:25–27, NASB; emphasis added).

When I came to this understanding, I thought my journey was over. I had found the answer to how the New Testament understood and applied the Old Testament in light of Jesus and his ministry. But I soon discovered a second and unexpected stage to my journey. If Israel is fulfilled in Jesus, what does that imply about how the Old Testament's teaching on Israel's future should be understood? Even more pressing, what does Jesus's use of typology suggest concerning the modern-day application of that key Old Testament verse about Israel—Genesis 12:3?

*Chapter Six*

# The Promise to Abraham Fulfilled

*If you belong to Christ,
then you are Abraham's seed,
and heirs according to the promise.*
GALATIANS 3:29

WHAT I LEARNED ABOUT JESUS'S FULFILLMENT of the Old Testament helped me grasp God's overall plan for bringing his goodness to the world, but it also raised an additional issue. If Jesus's typological fulfillment of the Old Testament explains the way the New Testament writers applied the Old Testament, what about the promise God gave to Abraham?

> The LORD had said to Abram, "Go from your country, your people and your father's household to the land I will show you.
> "I will make you into a great nation,
>     and I will bless you;
> I will make your name great,
>     and you will be a blessing.
> I will bless those who bless you,
>     and whoever curses you I will curse;
> and all peoples on earth
>     will be blessed through you."
> GENESIS 12:1–3

> The LORD appeared to Abram and said, "To your offspring I will give this land." (Genesis 12:7a)

God's threefold promise to Abraham *seems* so straightforward: his descendants would become a large nation (Genesis 12:2), all peoples would be blessed through his offspring (Genesis 12:3), and God would give them the land of Canaan—today's land of Israel—for their home (Genesis 12:7).

| The Promise | OT Fulfillment |
| --- | --- |
| A large nation (Gen. 12:2-3; 13:14-17; 15:5, 18-19; 17:1-12; 18:16-19; 22:15-18; 26:2-4, 23-24; 28:1-4, 13-15; 32:12; 35:11-12; 48:3) | The nation of Israel comes into existence (Gen. 46:3; Deut. 26:5). |
| All peoples blessed through Abraham and his "seed" or offspring (Gen. 12:2-3; 18:16-19; 22:15-18; 26:2-44; 28:13-15) | Israel serves as "a kingdom of priests and a holy nation" which represents God to the nations (Ex. 19:6; 34:10; Deut. 4:6-8). |
| The land (Gen. 12:7; 13:14-17; 15:18-19; 17:1-12; 22:15-18; 24:7; 26:2-4; 28:1-4, 13-15; 35:11-12; 48:3) | The Israelites conquer and occupy the land of Canaan (Josh. 21:43-45). |

Straightforward as it seems, though, understanding the New Testament's use of the Old Testament in general forces us to ask: is it possible that Genesis 12 could also be fulfilled in Jesus? Did the New Testament writers give any indication that they understood the promise to Abraham in that way?

## THE APOSTLES AND THE PROMISE TO ABRAHAM

In two of his letters the apostle Paul directly addresses the significance of the promise to Abraham in light of the coming of Jesus. His words on the subject are eye-opening.

When Paul writes to the Galatians, he specifically mentions the covenant that God made with Abraham. The overall purpose of Galatians 3 is to combat the legalism the Galatians had fallen into, but in the process Paul provides significant insights into the meaning and purpose of the Abrahamic covenant.

> Understand, then, that those who have faith are children of Abraham. Scripture foresaw that God would justify the Gentiles by faith,

and announced the gospel in advance to Abraham: "All nations will be blessed through you." So those who rely on faith are blessed along with Abraham, the man of faith. (Galatians 3:7–9)

With those words Paul expands the promise made to Abraham in Genesis 12. First, he says that the children of Abraham are not just Abraham's physical descendants, as they were in the Old Testament. Now, "those who have faith are children of Abraham" (Galatians 3:7). The issue is no longer one of biology but of faith. Second, Paul teaches that the promise to bless all peoples through Abraham has been achieved in the gospel of Jesus Christ. Later in the chapter, Paul explains that in more specific terms:

The promises were spoken to Abraham and to his seed. Scripture does not say "and to seeds," meaning many people, but "and to your seed," meaning one person, who is Christ. (Galatians 3:16)

In order to establish his point, Paul cites the precise wording of the promise—"*to your offspring* I will give this land" (Genesis 12:7, emphasis added). The Hebrew term for "offspring" is *seed*. It can carry either a singular or plural sense. (Think of how English uses the word *deer*. It can refer to either one deer or many deer.) Therefore, the promise about Abraham's "seed" can be applied in the Old Testament to all of Abraham's physical descendants, but with the coming of Jesus it is the singular meaning that rises to prominence. Paul focuses on that singular sense. The "seed" is Christ.

Then Paul does something even more surprising. He refers to non-Jewish believers in terms that, from an Old Testament perspective, apply only to Jews.

If you belong to Christ, then you are Abraham's seed, and heirs according to the promise. (Galatians 3:29)

Something extraordinary has occurred through Christ. People who are not biologically the descendants of Abraham can now be called "Abraham's seed." Even more surprising is that those people are said to be "heirs according to the promise." Through Christ, people who have no biological relationship to Abraham are entitled to the benefits of the promise that God made to Abraham in Genesis 12.

In his letter to the Romans, Paul again addresses the significance of the promise to Abraham in light of the coming of Christ.

> Therefore, the promise comes by faith, so that it may be by grace and may be guaranteed to all Abraham's offspring—not only to those who are of the law but also to those who have the faith of Abraham. He is the father of us all. As it is written: "I have made you a father of many nations." He is our father in the sight of God, in whom he believed—the God who gives life to the dead and calls into being things that were not. (Romans 4:16–17)

This passage repeats what Paul earlier wrote to the Galatians. The promise made to Abraham is no longer limited to those of biological descent. It is also given to those who have placed their faith in Christ. The promise to Abraham now applies to all Christians regardless of their ethnic background because the covenant with Abraham has found its fulfillment in Jesus Christ.

This understanding of God's promise to Abraham finds additional confirmation in the way that both Paul and Peter describe followers of Christ. In his letter to the Ephesians, Paul states that believers in Christ are not foreigners among God's people. They are "heirs together with Israel" (Ephesians 3:6). Paul elaborates on this theme:

> ...remember that at that time you were separate from Christ, excluded from citizenship in Israel and foreigners to the covenants of the promise, without hope and without God in the world. But now in Christ Jesus you who once were far away have been brought near by the blood of Christ....
>
> Consequently, you are no longer foreigners and strangers, but fellow citizens with God's people and also members of his household, built on the foundation of the apostles and prophets, with Christ Jesus himself as the chief cornerstone. (Ephesians 2:12–13, 19–20)

What an incredible development has taken place through Christ!

Believers from a non-Jewish background are "no longer foreigners and strangers, but fellow citizens."

The apostle Peter writes in a similar manner in his first letter. People who are not biological descendants of Abraham are described in terms that, in Exodus 19:5–6, applied solely to Abraham's physical offspring. Note the similarities between Peter's words and those found in Exodus.

> But you are a chosen people, *a royal priesthood, a holy nation, God's special possession*, that you may declare the praises of him who called you out of darkness into his wonderful light. Once you were not a people, but now you are the people of God; once you had not received mercy, but now you have received mercy. (1 Peter 2:9–10, emphasis added)

> Now if you obey me fully and keep my covenant, then out of all nations you will be *my treasured possession*. Although the whole earth is mine, you will be for me *a kingdom of priests* and *a holy nation*. (Exodus 19:5–6a, emphasis added)

It is startling how freely the apostles take Old Testament terminology and apply what was once limited to the Israelites to those who have trusted in Jesus Christ as Lord. How can they make such a free use of the Old Testament Scriptures? The answer is found in the earth-shaking and world-changing significance of Christ. All that God did beforehand through Israel cannot come close to what God did through his Son!

The example and teaching of Jesus and the letters by his apostles affirm the full significance and glory of Christ. In fact, he is the embodiment and fulfillment of Israel. What came before Christ was always designed to point to him.

> Therefore do not let anyone judge you by what you eat or drink, or with regard to a religious festival, a New Moon celebration or a Sabbath day. These are a shadow of the things that were to come; the reality, however, is found in Christ. (Colossians 2:16–17)

All of the Old Testament promises, including the one made to Abraham, have been completely fulfilled in "the reality" that is Christ himself!

## The New Testament and the Land

All Christians acknowledge some connection between the promise to Abraham and Christ, but is that connection as comprehensive as I have just explained? To put it simply: What about the land? God did promise Abraham and his descendants the land of Canaan. If the promise to Abraham was fulfilled in Jesus, was the territorial aspect of the promise also fulfilled? If so, how?

The promise of the land in the Old Testament and its significance in the New Testament needs to be considered carefully.[153] The fulfillment of the land promise in Jesus is not as immediately apparent as his fulfillment of the Sabbath or the temple or the Passover, but Jesus and his disciples *did* address the subject. Recall Jesus's teaching about rest in Matthew 11:28: "Come to me, all you who are weary and burdened, and I will give you rest." The promise of Sabbath rest in the Old Testament was fulfilled in Jesus. The Old Testament, however, did not limit rest to the Sabbath. Rest was also found in the land.

> But you will cross the Jordan and settle in the land the LORD your God is giving you as an inheritance, and he will give you *rest* from all your enemies around you so that you will live in safety. (Deuteronomy 12:10, emphasis added)

> Remember the command that Moses the servant of the LORD gave you after he said, "The LORD your God will give you *rest* by giving you this land." (Joshua 1:13, emphasis added)

> The LORD gave them *rest* on every side, just as he had sworn to their ancestors. Not one of their enemies withstood them; the LORD gave all their enemies into their hands. (Joshua 21:44, emphasis added)

> Praise be to the LORD, who has given *rest* to his people Israel just as he promised. Not one word has failed of all the good promises he gave through his servant Moses. (1 Kings 8:56, emphasis added)

In chapter 4 of Hebrews, the writer takes that Old Testament promise of rest in the land and applies it to Christ. There was a rest available in the land into which Joshua led the Israelites, but the writer to the Hebrews teaches that there was another rest to follow. That later rest comes through Jesus, so the writer urges the readers of his letter to make sure that they have entered that later rest:

> For if Joshua had given them rest, God would not have spoken later about another day… Let us, therefore, make every effort to enter that rest, so that no one will perish by following their example of disobedience. (Hebrews 4:9, 11)

Both Jesus's words and the teaching of Hebrews suggest that the concept of rest, which was such a central part of the Israelites' understanding of the land, is fulfilled in Jesus Christ.

There is still more on the subject of the land when the New Testament's complete teaching is examined. Consider what Paul writes to the Romans when discussing the promise to Abraham:

> It was not through the law that Abraham and his offspring received the promise that he would be heir of *the world*, but through the righteousness that comes by faith. (Romans 4:13, emphasis added)

Paul writes that Abraham and his descendants would inherit "the world," but where was that promise found in the Old Testament? In Genesis the promise was limited to the land of Canaan, but Paul expands the promise to the whole world.

Consider also the way that Paul slightly yet significantly changes one of the Ten Commandments. A comparison between the Old Testament's precise instruction and Paul's quotation of it reveals a noteworthy difference:

> Honor your father and your mother, as the LORD your God has commanded you, so that you may live long and that it may go well with you *in the land the LORD your God is giving you*. (Deuteronomy 5:16, emphasis added).

"Honor your father and mother"—which is the first commandment with a promise—"so that it may go well with you and that you may enjoy long life *on the earth*." (Ephesians 6:2–3, emphasis added)

Paul once again enlarges or globalizes the Old Testament's teaching. The promise in the Old Testament was limited to the land of Canaan, but in the New Testament it is expanded to include all of the world.

Chapter 11 of Hebrews picks up the promise of the land once again and applies it in a different direction:

> By faith Abraham, when called to go to a place he would later receive as his inheritance, obeyed and went, even though he did not know where he was going. By faith he made his home in the promised land *like a stranger in a foreign country*; he lived in tents, as did Isaac and Jacob, who were heirs with him of the same promise. For he was looking forward to the city with foundations, whose architect and builder is God. (Hebrews 11:8–10, emphasis added)

As wonderful as entering the Promised Land was, Abraham still considered himself "a stranger in a foreign country." He knew God would bring about an even greater fulfillment, so he looked beyond the physical land to the "city with foundations, whose architect and builder is God." In subsequent verses the writer to the Hebrews expands on that teaching:

> All these people were still living by faith when they died. They did not receive the things promised; they only saw them and welcomed them from a distance, admitting that they were foreigners and strangers on earth. People who say such things show that they are looking for a country of their own. If they had been thinking of the country they had left, they would have had opportunity to return. Instead, *they were longing for a better country—a heavenly one*. (Hebrews 11:13–16, emphasis added)

It was not just Abraham, Isaac, and Jacob who knew there was a further aspect to the promise of the land in the Old Testament. Other godly people

## The Promise to Abraham Fulfilled

knew the same. They too looked beyond life in Israel to the heavenly country they longed for.

Close study of the New Testament reveals that the promise of the land was not ignored by the apostles. That promise to Abraham has been fulfilled. Christ fulfills the promise by providing the ultimate rest that the Israelites found only partially in the Promised Land. The experience of that rest is not just for the physical descendants of Abraham but for all those who have trusted in Christ. For this reason Paul can expand statements about the land of Israel to the entire world. Furthermore, the New Testament teaches that the promise will find its ultimate fulfillment when Christians experience their eternal rest through Christ in the new heaven and earth.

| The Promise | OT Fulfillment | NT Fulfillment |
|---|---|---|
| **A large nation** (Gen. 12:2-3; 13:14-17; 15:5, 18-19; 17:1-2; 18:16-19; 22:15-18; 26:2-4, 23-24; 28:1-4, 13-15; 32:12; 35:11-12; 48:3) | The nation of Israel comes into existence (Gen. 46:3; Deut. 26:5). | Abraham is the "father of us all" or "the father of many nations" (Rom. 4:16-17). His offspring include those who have the faith of Abraham regardless of ethnic origin (Rom. 4:16). The children of Abraham are those who believe in Christ (Gal. 3:7). The blessing comes to the Gentiles through Christ Jesus (Gal. 3:14). |
| **All peoples blessed through Abraham and his "seed" or offspring** (Gen. 12:2-3; 18:16-19; 22:15-18; 26:2-44; 28:13-15) | Israel serves as "a kingdom of priests and a holy nation" who represent God to the nations (Ex. 19:6; 34:10; Deut. 4:6-8). | God announced the gospel to the Gentiles through this promise (Gal. 3:8). The "seed" is Christ (Gal. 3:16). |
| **The land** (Gen. 12:7; 13:14-17; 15:18-19; 17:1-12; 22:15-18; 24:7; 26:2-4; 28:1-4, 13-15; 35:11-12; 48:3) | The Israelites conquer and occupy the land of Canaan and experience God's rest (Josh. 21:43-45). | "Come to me, all you who are weary and burdened, and I will give you rest" (Matt. 11:28). Abraham and his offspring receive the promise that he would be heir of *the world*" (Rom. 4:13 emphasis added). "Honor your father and mother...that you may enjoy long life on *the earth*" (Eph. 6:2-3 emphasis added; compare to Deut. 5:16's "in *the land* the Lord your God is giving you"). "Abraham...was looking forward to the city with foundations, whose architect and builder is God...they were longing for a better country—a heavenly one" (Hebrews 11:10, 16). |

## An Everlasting Promise

But wait! Are we moving too quickly? The passages quoted above do indicate that there is a connection of some kind between the Old Testament promise of the land, the coming of Jesus Christ, the universal spread of the gospel, and the assurance of eternal life. But is connection necessarily the same as fulfillment? What about the promise that the land will be an "everlasting possession" of Abraham's biological descendants?

> The LORD said to Abram after Lot had parted from him, "Look around from where you are, to the north and south, to the east and west. All the land that you see I will give to you and your offspring *forever* [Hebrew *'ôlām*]. I will make your offspring like the dust of the earth, so that if anyone could count the dust, then your offspring could be counted. Go, walk through the length and breadth of the land, for I am giving it to you. (Genesis 13:14–17, emphasis added)

> I will establish my covenant as an *everlasting* [*'ôlām*] covenant between me and you and your descendants after you for the generations to come, to be your God and the God of your descendants after you. The whole land of Canaan, where you now reside as a foreigner, I will give as an *everlasting* [*'ôlām*] possession to you and your descendants after you; and I will be their God. (Genesis 17:7–8, emphasis added)

Perhaps Jesus, the gospel, and heaven can be viewed as fulfillments of the promise to Abraham, but should they really be understood as the complete and ultimate fulfillment? After all, an "everlasting possession" lasts forever. Don't the words used in the promise of the land indicate that they must still apply to the physical descendants of Abraham? Christian Zionist leader John Hagee points out that Deuteronomy 7:9 promises God's love to his people "for a thousand generations," and then explains:

> God keeps covenant for a thousand generations! Technically speak-

ing, a thousand generations is forty thousand years, but the reference is simply an expression of speech that emphasizes the meaning *forever*. God is a God of everlasting covenant. The God of Abraham, Isaac, and Jacob does not break covenant—*ever*![154]

At first glance this issue seems to be an open-and-shut case, but taking all of the Old Testament into account reveals that it is not as simple as it first appears. There are other aspects of God's covenant with Israel that were also described by the Hebrew word *'ôlām*, the term used in Genesis 13:15 and 17:7–8 and translated as "forever" or "everlasting." Investigation of those additional references to the covenant will shed light on how the Bible actually uses this term.

*'ôlām* was used to describe the Jewish feasts of Passover (Exodus 12:14, 17, 24), Firstfruits (Leviticus 23:14), Weeks (Leviticus 23:21), and Tabernacles (Leviticus 23:41). Each one of these feasts was declared to be "a lasting (*'ôlām*) ordinance for the generations to come." Yet Christians are not obligated to observe those feasts today. According to Colossians 2:17, those religious festivals "are a shadow of the things to come; the reality, however, is found in Christ."

Of greater significance was the application of *'ôlām* to the Old Testament commands about the priesthood of Aaron and his descendants:

> Then you shall take the anointing oil and pour it on [Aaron's] head and anoint him. You shall bring his sons and put tunics on them. You shall gird them with sashes, Aaron and his sons, and bind caps on them, and they shall have the priesthood by a perpetual [*'ôlām*] statute. (Exodus 29:7–9a, NASB)

The book of Leviticus also applied *'ôlām* to the instructions about the Day of Atonement:

> This shall be a permanent [*'ôlām*] statute for you: in the seventh month, on the tenth day of the month, you shall humble your souls and not do any work, whether the native, or the alien who sojourns among you; for it is on this day that atonement shall be

made for you to cleanse you; you will be clean from all your sins before the LORD. It is to be a sabbath of solemn rest for you, that you may humble your souls; it is a permanent [*ôlām*] statute. (Leviticus 16:29–31, NASB)

The use of *ôlām* in reference to Aaron and the Day of Atonement is particularly significant because the New Testament book of Hebrews—written to Jewish believers—declares that both of these have found their fulfillment in Christ. Hebrews compared the Old Testament priesthood to the new priesthood of Jesus:

> If perfection could have been attained through the Levitical priesthood—and indeed the law given to the people established that priesthood—*why was there still need for another priest to come*, one in the order of Melchizedek, not in the order of Aaron? For when *the priesthood is changed*, the law must be changed also. *He of whom these things are said belonged to a different tribe, and no one from that tribe has ever served at the altar.* For it is clear that our Lord descended from Judah, and in regard to that tribe Moses said nothing about priests. (Hebrews 7:11–14, emphasis added)

When compared to the teaching of the Old Testament about Aaron's priesthood being a perpetual or permanent [*ôlām*] statute, the teaching of Hebrews is breathtaking: "The priesthood is changed." How can this New Testament book make such a stunning declaration? The answer is simple: Jesus. His priestly superiority makes the previous priesthood unnecessary.

> …Jesus has become the guarantor of a better covenant. Now there have been many of those priests, since death prevented them from continuing in office; but because Jesus lives forever, he has a permanent priesthood. Therefore he is able to save completely those who come to God through him, because he always lives to intercede for them. (Hebrews 7:22–25)

The writer to the Hebrews continues with that same line of reasoning when examining the Old Testament law's instructions about the annual Day of Atonement.

> Nor did [Christ] enter heaven to offer himself again and again, the way the high priest enters the Most Holy Place every year with blood that is not his own. Otherwise Christ would have had to suffer many times since the creation of the world. But *he has appeared once for all* at the culmination of the ages to do away with sin by the sacrifice of himself. (Hebrews 9:25–26, emphasis added)

> Day after day every priest stands and performs his religious duties; again and again he offers the same sacrifices, which can never take away sins. But when this priest [Christ] had offered *for all time one sacrifice for sins*, he sat down at the right hand of God. (Hebrews 10:11–12, emphasis added)

The superiority of Christ changes the way the Old Testament is applied. The everlasting covenant finds its fulfillment in Christ. He completes God's purpose for the priesthood and the Day of Atonement. Aaron's priesthood and the Day of Atonement are no longer needed because they have been totally fulfilled through Christ and his sacrifice on the cross.

Careful study of the Old and New Testaments demonstrate that it is better to understand the Hebrew term *'ôlām* in a less absolute sense than the English words "forever" and "everlasting." The term is better interpreted as describing something that is of "indefinite continuance into the very distant future."[155] Practices that are described in the Old Testament as *'ôlām* may last a long time, but they do not necessarily continue into perpetuity or apply in the future in exactly the same way they did before.

First Samuel 2:30 confirms this conclusion about the use of *'ôlām*. Through a prophet God declared to the priest Eli, "'I promised that members of your family would minister before me forever [*'ôlām*].' But now the LORD declares: 'Far be it from me! Those who honor me I will honor, but those who despise me will be disdained.'" Even though the descendants of Eli had been promised the priesthood in perpetuity, they lost that privilege when the priesthood was transferred to the family of Zadok (1 Kings 2:27).

Those who insist that *'ôlām* means "everlasting" or "forever" in an absolute sense must also consider the implications of the judgment on Judah pronounced by Jeremiah in the late seventh century BC.

> But my people have forgotten me....
> making their land a horror, a thing to be hissed at forever [*'ôlām*].
> Jeremiah 18:15–16a, ESV

If *'ôlām* means "forever" in an absolute sense, then it follows that the land of Israel should now and forever be considered an object of scorn. (See also Isaiah 32:14, Psalm 74:3.) Are Christians who insist on interpreting *'ôlām* as meaning "forever" willing to adopt that attitude toward modern Israel?

Just as the "lasting ordinances" of the Old Testament law are fulfilled in Christ, so the "forever" and "everlasting" nature of the promise concerning the land is fulfilled in Christ. The monumental significance of Jesus Christ cannot be overemphasized!

## ONLY A SHADOW

Taking the entire teaching of the Old and New Testaments together leads to the conclusion that every aspect of the promise made to Abraham has been fulfilled in Christ. To apply the promise of Genesis 12:3 to the modern nation of Israel takes away from God's miraculous and superior work in his Son.

It must be remembered that the culmination of the promise to Abraham in Genesis 12:3 was not ultimately about Israel but about the world: "And all peoples on earth will be blessed through you" (Genesis 12:3b, Acts 3:25). God made a promise to bless the Israelites so that his favor and goodness could then be extended to all people. Israel was not the final destination of God's blessing; rather, it was God's vehicle designed to deliver God's goodness to the entire world. That global blessing came in Jesus Christ, and it explains why Jesus commissioned his disciples to "go and make disciples of all nations" (Matthew 28:19).

Paul and the writer of Hebrews agree on the colossal impact that Christ has produced in the world. Paul writes in Colossians 2:16–17 that the Old

Testament laws "are a shadow of the things that were to come; the reality, however, is found in Christ." Hebrews makes the same point. "The law is only a shadow of the good things that are coming—not the realities themselves" (Hebrews 10:1a).

Imagine looking at a lightbulb that has been turned on when the sun is shining brightly. The lightbulb's illumination is so overpowered by the sun's brilliant light that it is virtually invisible.[156] So it is with the everlasting promise God made to Abraham. The covenant with Abraham was crucial to the Old Testament, but it has been fulfilled and surpassed by God's work in Christ.

A simple but searching question must now be asked: Why do many evangelical Christians today concentrate so much attention on Israel when the New Testament teaches that Israel has been fulfilled in Jesus Christ? Why concentrate on the shadow instead of the reality? As the previous chapters have demonstrated, the answer lies in a mix of history and theology. Bible prophecy also fuels American evangelicals' unreserved support for Israel. It is to that subject that we now turn.

## Chapter Seven
# What about Bible Prophecy?

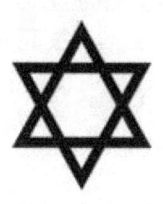

*The simple believe anything,
but the prudent give thought to their steps.*

PROVERBS 14:15

DURING THE WORSHIP SERVICE we had taken time to pray for the Christians living in Egypt. After the service a woman approached me with a smile and said, "I'm so glad we prayed for Egypt. Isn't it exciting to see what is happening in the Middle East? I don't know how all of it is going to work out, but we know that God has his hand on Israel. When I listen to the news, I can't help but think that Jesus is going to return soon!"

Few subjects create more excitement among evangelical Christians than the idea that God's predictions about the future are coming true in our own time. For over one hundred years now, prophecy teachers have highlighted the importance of Israel as the key to the future. William Blackstone wrote in his 1898 bestseller, *Jesus Is Coming*, that Israel "is God's sundial. If we want to know our place in the chronology, our position in the march of events, look at Israel."[157] Over a hundred years later, Walter Kaiser, an Old Testament scholar, repeated that advice: "If we wish to know where we are in the prophetic calendar, we need to keep our eyes on Israel, for they are God's timepiece."[158]

In the early 1970s I had an unquenchable desire to learn more about what God had planned for his world. I remember going to hear Hal Lindsey speak. The auditorium was packed with an eager audience. Lindsey explained how the events prophesied in the Old Testament were being fulfilled. Christ's second coming was obviously near!

Ever since then, I have been studying the subject of Bible prophecy. I've studied the Bible prophecies themselves—after all, that is the obvious place to start! I have also been drawn into a study of prophecy teachers like Hal Lindsey, Tim LaHaye, and Joel Rosenberg. That has proven to be almost as engrossing as the prophecies themselves. In the process, four major flaws in modern-day prophecy teaching have emerged.

## Flaw #1: "Prophecy for Dummies"

Most contemporary prophecy teachers make it appear that understanding the Bible's prophecies is relatively simple. Tim LaHaye assures his readers that "prophecy is just not that difficult." He explains:

> Often, laypeople who buy prophetic books or attend prophecy conferences or subscribe to prophetic magazines know more about the prophetic portions of the Scriptures than do their pastors....
>
> Anyone can understand the major events of Bible prophecy if they spend a little time comparing Scripture with Scripture.[159]

When Bible prophecy first grabbed my attention, I decided that I wanted to study the prophecies for myself. As a young Christian I had learned not to take someone else's word for what the Bible teaches. Instead, Christians should study the Bible for themselves. Looking up the Bible passages that Hal Lindsey referred to in *The Late Great Planet Earth*, I soon discovered the prophecies were not as easy to understand as Lindsey had made them out to be.

For example, prophecy teachers tend to base a lot of their teaching on the details of Revelation. They seem to know exactly what all those strange images symbolize, and they can explain precisely how all the details fit together and are going to be fulfilled. It's amazing how definite they are in their interpretation of the details of Revelation. Yet serious students of the Bible propose four major interpretative approaches to Revelation. Some think the prophecy of Revelation was fulfilled in the first century. Others see the fulfillment as happening throughout church history. Some say that

Revelation's predictions are yet to be fulfilled, and still others say that John's book speaks in general allegorical terms and cannot be limited to any one time frame. How can today's prophecy teachers be so dogmatic about passages that Christians equally committed to the inspiration of the Bible interpret in more than one way?[160]

Ezekiel 38 and 39 are two chapters of the Bible that contemporary prophecy teachers emphasize because they are understood as a prediction concerning Russia and its future invasion of Israel. Tim LaHaye says that these two chapters "are among the most specific and easy to understand in the prophetic word."[161] He neglects to mention that evangelical scholars disagree. Peter Craigie says, "The series of prophecies concerning Gog . . . are among the most difficult parts of the entire book of Ezekiel to interpret."[162] Even those who follow the same basic outline of end-time events do not agree on the time of Ezekiel 38 and 39's fulfillment. Will it be before, during, or after the tribulation? Or will it be after the millennium? Advocates for each position can be found.[163]

Ezekiel 40 through 48 seem to be more straightforward. It appears obvious that the prophet is predicting a future reconstruction of the temple in Jerusalem. But these chapters present their own set of problems. Daniel Block writes in his commentary on Ezekiel that "few sections of the book have yielded such a wide range of interpretations."[164] Scholars who are dedicated to the inspiration of the Bible have arrived at different interpretations. Some understand these chapters as describing a temple that Ezekiel expected the exiles to build when they returned from the Babylonian captivity. Others see the temple as a symbolic representation of Christ or his church, while many understand Ezekiel to be describing a temple that is yet to be built.

The major difficulty comes with the sacrifices described in Ezekiel 40, 43, and 46. If these chapters are interpreted to mean that a physical temple will be built in the future, then what function do the animal sacrifices have in light of the insistence found in the New Testament book of Hebrews that the sacrifice of Jesus was "once for all" (Hebrews 7:28; 9:12, 26; 10:12–14)?

There is one other prophecy that is frequently cited as foundational for understanding what God has in store for Israel. Daniel 9 is central to much modern-day prophecy teaching. This is the passage that is cited as evidence that the temple in Jerusalem will be rebuilt and that the Antichrist will make a covenant with Israel which he will then break after three and a half years.

Most popular books on the end times present Daniel's prophecy about the seventy weeks as a straightforward and easily understandable teaching that every sincere Bible student agrees on. But research in a detailed commentary on Daniel proves otherwise. In fact, Christian scholars who believe firmly in the inspiration of the Bible have come to different conclusions about the seventy weeks. Daniel 9:24–27 has been called the "Dismal Swamp" of Old Testament studies.[165] Bible scholars for at least fifteen centuries have struggled to understand this passage. Jerome (c. A.D. 345–c. 419) said:

> I realize that this question has been argued over in various ways by men of greatest learning.... And so, because it is unsafe to pass judgment upon the opinions of the great teachers of the Church and set one above another, I shall simply repeat the view of each, and leave it to the reader's judgment as to whose explanation ought to be followed.[166]

One twentieth-century commentator writes:

> The difficulty of the verses which now lie before us is evident to anyone who has even attempted a cursory examination of them... Pick up almost any two commentaries from the same school of eschatology and it is not likely that there will be agreement on the meaning of all the details of interpretation.[167]

Should we build a chronology of future events on such a difficult passage?

Prior to 1948, students of prophecy debated the sequence of events leading to Israel's restoration. In the nineteenth century, prophecy teachers overwhelmingly believed that the Jews would not return to their ancient land until after the second coming of Christ. With the start of the Zionist movement under Herzl, however, Bible teachers started to take a different approach: the Jews' return to the land would take place prior to Christ's return. Then a new issue started to be debated. Some prophecy teachers asserted that Israel would return to the land before they had trusted in Christ, but others maintained that the restoration to the land would only come after they had turned to Christ.[168]

Reading contemporary prophecy literature, Christians today would hardly know that such a debate even took place. After 1948, popular prophecy teachers began to state without hesitation that the Bible presents Israel's return to the land as occurring in a state of unbelief. Marvin Rosenthal says, "The Bible is clear: Israel's physical restoration to the land must precede her spiritual regeneration in the land (Ezekiel 37:14)."[169] The International Christian Embassy in Jerusalem agrees. "Ezek 36:24-28 is very clear that their return is just the beginning: first there is a physical return and then there is a spiritual restoration."[170]

It's amazing that prophecy teachers can develop elaborate and intricate chronologies about end-time events and write book after book suggesting that these prophecies are on the verge of being fulfilled without even hinting at the possibility that they may be wrong. They rarely if ever tell their readers that they are basing many of their major ideas on passages that are difficult to understand.[171]

In his second New Testament letter, the apostle Peter admits that there are some things in Paul's writings that are hard to understand (2 Peter 3:16). If Peter can say that about Paul, then why should evangelicals be hesitant to make the same admission when it comes to some biblical prophecies? Christians who are equally committed to the inspiration and authority of the Bible have come to different conclusions about what those prophecies teach. Why not openly admit it?

## Flaw #2: Jumping to Conclusions

One of the reasons Bible prophecy is so exciting is that it seems so incredibly contemporary. We are told that events taking place in the Middle East today are predicted in God's Word. Prophets from centuries ago are presented as providing Christians with divine insight into the present circumstances of Israel and the surrounding region.

But that is precisely the problem: Today's prophecy teachers move too quickly. They jump to conclusions. They take words written over two thousand years ago and then jump to the contemporary scene so fast that they omit any discussion of what the prophet's message would have meant to the people who first heard the prophecies. Prophecy teachers need to slow down! The ancient prophets of Israel did not write their messages with twenty-first-century readers in mind. Christians today can certainly learn from their ancient writings, but it must be remembered that the prophets originally delivered their prophecies to the people of their own day. In *Basic Bible Interpretation*, Roy Zuck explains one of the first principles of Bible study:

> *Each biblical writing was written by someone to specific hearers or readers in a specific historical, geographical situation for a specific purpose*...exegesis [interpretation] is to discover the original meaning of the text. In other words what were the words conveying to their initial readers? Before we can determine their significance or relevance to us today, people who are not the original readers, we must first seek to determine what the words meant to those who originally read them.[172]

When reading the Bible's prophetic writings, this principle requires us to first understand what a prophet's message would have meant to his contemporaries. Unfortunately the prophecy "experts" ignore that basic principle.

Consider Tim LaHaye's comments on Ezekiel 37, the famous chapter about the valley of the dry bones. Ezekiel was given that vision in order to demonstrate how God was going to bring his people back to their homeland. LaHaye interprets the vision solely in terms of the events of 1948 when the modern nation of Israel came into existence.[173] He never mentions that Ezekiel 37 might have contained a message for the people who were living in exile in Babylon when Ezekiel originally gave the prophecy. Could it be that the prophecy of the dry bones was fulfilled not in 1948 but in 539 BC when the Israelites returned to their homeland? LaHaye never even asks that question.

Think about the book of Revelation, which captures our attention because of its vivid and puzzling images. We immediately want to know what the seals and trumpets and bowls represent. When a prophecy teacher interprets them for us in terms of contemporary military technology or present-day political realities, Revelation becomes even more fascinating. But John wrote Revelation for Christians living in the first century. Those Christians were being persecuted by the Roman Empire for their faith in Jesus. So the first question to be asked is how those early Christians would have understood the book of Revelation.

If Revelation is only a description of events in the far distant future, what relevance would it have had for the early Christians, who needed a message to encourage them in their immediate circumstances? How would a description of events in the twenty-first century have helped the early Christians? When reading Revelation, we should start by asking what the terms and images meant to the first-century Christians who were being persecuted by the Romans. That's not necessarily easy to figure out. It's more exciting to jump right to the twenty-first century, but we must resist that urge no matter how strong it is. First we should think through the message of Revelation for the early Christians and only then think about how that message applies to Christians today.

This guideline for Bible study is so crucial that we need to consider one more example. In Matthew 24 and 25 we find Jesus's most extensive teaching about future events. Standing on the Mount of Olives, Jesus describes in Matthew 24:4–14 how false prophets will claim to be the Christ and how Christians will be persecuted for their faith. Wars and famines and earthquakes will also occur. Verses 15 through 21 contain instructions to his followers to flee from Jerusalem when they see certain events take place. Many prophecy teachers say that the predictions of verses 4–14 will be fulfilled in the period leading up to the seven-year tribulation before Christ's return and that verses 15 through 21 apply to the tribulation itself.[174]

The problem with that interpretation becomes apparent when we ask whether the disciples who were with Jesus on the Mount of Olives would have understood his words that way. How would they have known that Jesus was talking about what would happen to a future generation of Christians instead of what would happen to them? In fact, wouldn't it have been natural for them to have thought their Master's teaching applied to them?

Jesus answered, "Watch out that no one deceives you. For many will come in my name, claiming 'I am the Christ,' and will deceive many. You will hear of wars and rumors of wars, but see to it that you are not alarmed. Such things must happen, but the end is still to come." (Matthew 24:4–6)

When the disciples standing on the Mount of Olives with Jesus heard him say, "you will hear of wars and rumors of wars," they would naturally have concluded that he was referring to what they should expect in their lifetimes. To take the entire passage as applying to a distant generation, as prophecy teachers today are in the habit of doing, is to make Jesus's teaching irrelevant to the disciples who first heard his words.

Questions have to be asked. Why do today's prophecy "experts" not follow a proper approach toward interpreting the prophecies of the Bible? Why do they jump to conclusions?

## Flaw #3: Here We Go Again

As we've seen, a major part of the fascination Christians have with Bible prophecy stems from its apparent relevance to the events of today. According to contemporary prophecy teachers, we are able to see how current events fit exactly into God's plan that was revealed centuries ago!

There is a flaw in that line of reasoning that must not be overlooked. We are not the only Christians who have thought that the ancient prophecies of the Bible were being fulfilled in their lifetimes. In fact, almost every generation of Christians has thought it was living in the final days before Christ's second coming.[175]

In AD 378, the Goths annihilated the Roman emperor's army. In response, Ambrose, Bishop of Milan, proclaimed that "the end of the world is coming upon us."[176] Another early church leader, Apollinarius, arrived at 482 as the date for the second coming of Christ; he based his calculation on the sixty-two "sevens" of Daniel 9:26.[177] John Milton, author of *Paradise Lost*, witnessed England's civil war from 1642 to 1660 and concluded that Jesus would return soon. The Puritan preacher John Cotton predicted 1655 as the year when the Antichrist's power would end. The following year, 1656, was Christopher Columbus's prediction for the end of the world.

John Napier, the inventor of logarithms, used his new mathematical technique to compute 1688 as the date for Christ's return. Cotton Mather, another Puritan preacher, predicted 1697 as the date of the end. Later he decided it would be 1736, but he eventually moved his predicted date back to 1716.[178] In the nineteenth century, William Miller gained a huge following by predicting that Jesus would return sometime between March 21, 1843 and March 21, 1844. When that prediction failed, he arrived at October 22, 1844 as the time for Christ's second coming.[179] In all of these cases, Christians arrived at their conclusions using methods of Bible interpretation much like the ones that evangelical Christians commonly use today.

In Ezekiel 38, two nations named Gog and Gomer form an alliance. Prophecy teachers in the 1930s determined that those two nations were none other than Russia and Germany. It was hard to believe that Nazi Germany could enter into an alliance with communist Russia. After all, they were sworn enemies. But on August 23, 1939, Hitler and Stalin did sign a nonaggression pact. The prophecy teachers were elated because Ezekiel 38 was being fulfilled. But in June of 1941 Hitler broke the treaty and launched a massive attack on Russia.[180] The prophecy teachers had to withdraw their predictions.

Those are just a few of the many mistakes that have been made by Christians through the centuries. They all had their reasons for believing they were living at the end of history, and they were all wrong. At the very least, this history lesson should make Christians pause before confidently asserting that the "signs of the times" point to the Lord's soon return. C.S. Lewis offers a wise alternative: "As a Christian I take it for granted that human history will some day end; and I am offering Omniscience no advice as to the best date for that consummation."[181] Believers in Jesus can and should look forward to Christ's return, but they should exercise extreme caution in predicting when his return will be.

History teaches us another bitter lesson. Prophecy teachers have not only made erroneous predictions. When those predictions have failed, they have gone on to make additional predictions instead of entirely renouncing the temptation to forecast the future.

Hal Lindsey is a good example. In his 1970 bestseller *The Late Great*

*Planet Earth*, he wrote, "Since the restoration of Israel in 1948, we have lived in the most significant period of prophetic history."[182] But in 1996 he wrote another book, *Planet Earth—A.D. 2000*. He had obviously changed his mind: "As I have restudied the Book of Daniel recently, I have begun to see that the recapture of Jerusalem [in 1967] was much more important than even the taking and reestablishing of the nation of Israel."[183]

That wasn't the only thing Lindsey changed. In his first book he wrote, "It is obvious that the real leader in the Arabic world is Egypt." Yet twenty-six years later he didn't mention Egypt at all. Instead he described Iran as "the leader of the new Islamic world order."[184]

Questions naturally arise. If Lindsey was mistaken about the importance of 1948 and the role of Egypt, then isn't it possible that some of his other teachings were wrong? Why should his readers have any confidence in his latest version of future events?

There was one thing, however, that Hal Lindsey remained firm on. In both his 1970 and 1996 books, he taught about what he called a "Revived Roman Empire."[185] In the end times there would be a confederation of ten European nations headquartered in Rome. But in 1999 Tim LaHaye wrote *Are We Living in the End Times?* and disagreed with Lindsey. LaHaye taught that the ten nations described in Bible prophecy need not be limited to Europe, and he said nothing about a revived Roman Empire. Instead, he taught that there would be ten administrative regions to a world government that was centered not in Rome but in the rebuilt city of Babylon.[186] How could Hal Lindsey and Tim LaHaye, two of the most famous prophecy "experts" in North America today, have come to such different interpretations of Bible prophecy?

It's worth noting that Tim LaHaye has also changed his teaching over the years. In 1972 he wrote a book titled *The Beginning of the End*. He said that the first sign of the end times was World War I. He predicted that some of the people who were alive in 1914 would see the fulfillment of all the end-time events. In 1991, LaHaye revised the book and changed the key date from 1914 to 1948. Now it was the generation alive when Israel became a modern nation that would see the fulfillment of the end times. In that revised edition, Tim LaHaye didn't explain the change. In fact, he never even mentioned that he had changed his teaching.[187] One suspects it had more to do with the rapidly aging 1914 generation than it did with a change in the Bible's teachings.

Historian Timothy Weber comments on the tendency of Christians to listen to the popular prophecy teachers in spite of their ongoing mistakes:

> In retrospect, premillennialists had shown more enthusiasm than accuracy in their interpretations.... Their leaders were confident *that* biblical prophecy was being fulfilled, but events kept forcing them to reevaluate their interpretations of how it was being fulfilled. One is struck by how forgiving and forgetful the...rank and file must have been during this period. They stuck by their leaders even when they misread the signs of the times. The leaders themselves seemed little deterred by their mistakes. Events were changing so quickly that they had little time for apologies....
>
> Some of the movement's most respected teachers, not just a lonely eccentric here and there, have been "made ridiculous by current history".... They presented themselves as students of the "sure word of prophecy" who claimed to have an infallible guide for the unraveling of future events. No...Bible scholar claimed omniscience for his interpretations, but few showed much humility or tentativeness either.[188]

Another historian, Paul Boyer, makes a similar observation about the remarkable way that prophecy teachers can get away with changing their interpretations.

> For prophecy to confirm the fundamentalist view of biblical inerrancy, its precise "fit" with historical reality had to be maintained—a feat that required constant adjustment and ingenuity. While the core structure of the premillennial scenario remained remarkably stable for 150 years, new events were continually elevated to the status of "prophetic fulfillments" or "end-time signs" while individuals or events that failed to live up to their expected role were quietly dropped....
>
> The historian, reading hundreds of prophecy books published

over a two-hundred-year period, can readily see this process of inserting current events into an archaic belief system. The average believer, encountering the genre for the first time, may be stunned by the uncanny contemporaneity of the prophecies.[189]

History shows all too convincingly that Christians are prone to be overly enthusiastic in identifying current events with the fulfillment of biblical prophecy. When the same mistakes are made by generation after generation of Christians, it is time to call nonsense by its name. Self-proclaimed prophecy "experts" simply don't possess the expertise that they and their followers think they do.

In 1870, George Müller, the famous English preacher best known for his founding of orphanages and his life of faith, warned his generation against overconfidence in promoting detailed schemes about the future:

> We should not be too hasty in forming a judgment that because a certain event has taken place, therefore at a particular time it is certain the Lord Jesus will return. Otherwise, when the time shall have passed…unbelievers may turn round and say, "The time has passed, and the Lord Jesus, of Whose return you talked so much, has not come.… We should be careful not to give a handle to those who speak evil of the truth."

That's a warning that the present generation of Christians needs to heed as well.[190]

Instead of surrendering to our own gullibility, evangelical Christians need to be cautious when digesting the latest batch of popular prophecy teaching. "The simple believe anything, but the prudent give thought to their steps" (Proverbs 14:15). History provides ample reason to exercise restraint and caution when it comes to asserting that present-day events are the fulfillment of biblical prophecies.

## FLAW #4: MISSING THE POINT

The fourth and most serious flaw in modern prophecy teaching is the way that the ethical dimension of prophecy is overlooked. Students of the Bible should first recognize that predictions about the future do not necessarily justify any action connected to the fulfillment of that prophecy. In other words, genuine prophecies from God can be misused.

Second Kings 9 records the story of how Elisha sent a divine message to Jehu in 841 BC. God declared to Jehu, "You are to destroy the house of Ahab your master, and I will avenge the blood of my servants the prophets and the blood of all the Lord's servants shed by Jezebel" (2 Kings 9:7). Jehu wasted no time in traveling to Jezreel, where he killed Jehoram, king of Israel, and his mother, Jezebel, who had promoted the worship of the idol Baal. But Jehu did not stop with those killings. Without any further instruction from God, he proceeded to assassinate Ahaziah, king of Judah, along with forty-two members of his family.

Approximately eighty-five years later, the prophet Hosea was given instructions on naming his son. "The Lord said to Hosea, 'Call him Jezreel, because I will soon punish the house of Jehu for the massacre at Jezreel'" (Hosea. 1:4a). Jehu had received a genuine instruction from God but had misinterpreted and misused it. D.A. Carson comments, "The lesson is important. Not even divine prophecy frees a person from the obligations of morality, integrity, and loyal and obedient faith in God. The end does not justify the means."[191]

That remains true today. Even if the establishment of modern Israel should be understood as the fulfillment of Old Testament prophecies, that does not provide justification for the way the Israeli government is treating the Palestinians under its control. Just as God held Jehu accountable for his misapplication of a legitimate prophecy, so God will hold modern Israel accountable for the injustices it is currently inflicting on Palestinians.

Those who appeal to Bible prophecy to explain their unqualified support for Israel appear to be blind to the ultimate purpose of prophecy. Part of the problem arises from our English language. To many people, a prophecy is defined simply as a prediction. Therefore, a prophet is obviously someone who explains what will happen in the future. But the English word *prophet* comes from the Greek verb *propheō*, which means "to speak for." In the Bible a prophet is someone who "speaks for" God, not necessarily someone who makes predictions.

Contrary to the way that Bible prophecy is commonly presented, the purpose of prophecy is not to predict but to persuade.[192] Read the Old Testament prophets. How many predictions do they actually make? What do the Old Testament prophets emphasize? Is their focus on future events, or do the prophets spend most of their time trying to persuade the people of their day to live for God instead of for themselves?

I remember the first time I read through the Old Testament prophets. To be frank, I was disappointed. Early in my Christian life I had been given the impression that the prophets made all kinds of fascinating predictions about what was going on in the Middle East today. But when I actually read the prophets for myself, I couldn't find many predictions at all. The ones I did find were not nearly as understandable as some people suggested they were. The Old Testament prophets simply did not live up to my expectations.

In 1971 the Jerusalem Conference on Biblical Prophecy brought together leading evangelical scholars to explore the modern relevance of the Bible's prophecies. The conference included one Israeli scholar, R.J. Zwi Werblowsky, a professor at the Hebrew University in Jerusalem, who spoke on the Israeli view of prophecy:

> Most of us do not regard prophecy as prediction. We do not believe that the significance of the Biblical message is in its capacity to foretell events or to provide a timetable for the happenings of tomorrow.... In fact, to many of us the very idea that prophecy is prediction would appear to be a diminution of the actual spiritual stature and spiritual significance of the prophetic message.[193]

The Old Testament prophet Amos provides a good example. Over 58 percent of Amos is composed of predictions,[194] but statistics do not tell the whole story. First, the predictions are rarely specific. A prophecy in Amos 5 is typical:

> "Therefore I will send you into exile beyond Damascus,"
>     says the LORD, whose name is God Almighty.
> AMOS 5:27

## What about Bible Prophecy?

That is a prediction, but is it specific? What did it mean that the people of Israel were going to be exiled "beyond Damascus"? A quick look at a map indicates that there is a lot of land east of the city of Damascus. There's Iraq and Iran and India. Even China could be described as "beyond Damascus." Furthermore, Amos did not give any indication of when this exile was going to take place. Was God going to send them into exile right away, or was it a matter of a few years or even a few decades before that was going to happen? Amos did not say. This prediction—like most of Amos's predictions and most of the Old Testament's predictions—was general.

Of course, there are exceptions. The prophet Jeremiah gave a specific prediction that the Jews would be exiled to Babylonia for seventy years (Jeremiah 25:11–12), and Daniel made some specific predictions in chapter 11 of his book.[195] But those are the exceptions rather than the rule.

Second, the predictions are always intended to reinforce the persuasion. Prediction and persuasion work together. They are not two entirely different things. It's not as if Amos said, "I have just received from God a very interesting prediction about the future." And then sometime later on he added, "I have also received a message from God about how he wants you to live." That is not the way the Old Testament prophets spoke. Instead they tied prediction and persuasion together. Look again at the prediction in Amos,

> "You have lifted up the shrine of your king,
>     The pedestal of your idols,
>     The star of your god—
>     Which you made for yourselves.
> Therefore I will send you into exile beyond Damascus,"
>     says the LORD, whose name is God Almighty.
> AMOS 5:26–27

In that prophecy God was making a prediction about a future trek to Damascus because he was trying to persuade his people to repent of their idolatry. If they did not obey, they would be sent "into exile beyond Damascus." To be forcefully taken from home and made into a refugee in a foreign land was something to avoid at all costs. That was the message Amos was delivering. The prediction was intended to reinforce the persuasion.

God made a prediction through his prophet in order to persuade the people to repent of their sinful actions and turn back to the way God wanted them to live.

The four flaws of modern prophecy teaching provide a strong warning against treating the message of the Old Testament prophets as nothing more than predictions about things happening today. But two important questions can be raised about the approach to Bible prophecy presented in this chapter.

*Question #1: What about Unfulfilled Old Testament Prophecy?*

First, what should Christians do with the Old Testament prophecies that have yet to be fulfilled? Shouldn't those prophecies be understood literally? Would not understanding them in any other way be an example of distorting God's unchanging truth?

In light of the New Testament, it's worth asking whether we should actually understand these prophecies as unfulfilled. A prophecy found in Amos 9 is instructive. Amos warned his ninth-century BC contemporaries of the judgment God would bring upon their nation if they did not repent. At the end of his book, however, Amos promised that even after the judgment, God would restore his people.

> "In that day
>
> "I will restore David's fallen shelter—
>     I will repair its broken walls
>     and restore its ruins—
>     and will rebuild it as it used to be,
> so that they may possess the remnant of Edom
>     and all the nations that bear my name,"
> declares the LORD, who will do these things.
>     AMOS 9:11–12

The meaning of those verses seems straightforward. God said that sometime after the Israelites were carried off into exile, they would be restored as a nation and regain their place of prominence in the Middle

East. The humbled nation of Israel, "David's fallen shelter," would be restored to its previous prominence. It would even rule over the neighboring nation of Edom as it had when David was on the throne.

In the New Testament book of Acts, this very passage from Amos was quoted during the meeting in Jerusalem when the apostles were seeking God's wisdom about the place of Gentiles in the community of Christian disciples.

> The whole assembly became silent as they listened to Barnabas and Paul telling about the signs and wonders God had done among the Gentiles through them. When they finished, James spoke up. "Brothers," he said, "listen to me. Simon has described to us how God first intervened to choose a people for his name from the Gentiles. The words of the prophets are in agreement with this, as it is written:
> "'After this I will return
> and rebuild David's fallen tent.
> Its ruins I will rebuild,
> and I will restore it,
> that the rest of mankind may seek the Lord,
> even all the Gentiles who bear my name,
> says the Lord, who does these things'—
> things known from long ago."
> ACTS 15:12–18

James cited this prophecy of Amos in order to demonstrate to the other Christians gathered in Jerusalem that salvation through Christ was not limited to the Jews. God's love extended to those who were not biological descendants of Abraham. For these early apostles, possessing "the remnant of Edom" was understood to teach that Gentiles could become followers of Christ in the same way that Jews could.

The question must be asked whether any Israelite living in Amos's day would have drawn a similar application. Unlikely, to say the least! Yet James used this prophecy as justification for receiving non-Jews into the fellowship of believers. How could he do such a thing? James's application of this Old

Testament prophecy demonstrates how Jesus changes the application of Old Testament truth. David's royal descendant rebuilt the people of God in a way that far exceeded the understanding of the prophet Amos. God had ultimately fulfilled Israel's mission work through Jesus Christ and produced a people that included believers from every ethnic background.

Other Old Testament prophecies should be understood in the same way. For example, Ezekiel 40 through 48 describes a temple in the land of Israel. That temple has yet to be built. Should Christians look forward to its future construction?

Ezekiel 40 through 48 was originally given to the exiles living in Babylon in the sixth century BC in order to persuade them that God was not finished with them even though he had judged them for their persistent disobedience. There would come a time when the holy worship of the one true God of Israel would be restored. God's people would once again live under his loving rule in the land he had chosen for them. The purpose of the prophecy was to persuade them to maintain their hope and faith, not to predict for them exactly how God's loving promises would be fulfilled.

So how should Christians think of the present-day significance of Ezekiel's temple vision? The New Testament indicates it was fulfilled in Christ. Jesus was the embodiment of the Old Testament tabernacle (John 1:14) and temple (Matthew 12:8). He taught that he was the location of true worship (John 4:19–26). The streams of living water that flowed from Ezekiel's temple (Ezekiel 47:1–12) came ultimately from Jesus (John 7:37–39).

Christopher Wright captures the idea well:

> Jesus Christ has taken on the full theological and spiritual significance of all that land, city and temple had for Israel and opened that significance up to people of all nations. In the light of this it seems...that Christian interpretations of Ezekiel which insist that there will be yet a literal and physical fulfillment of his vision by the actual building of another temple in Jerusalem, with accompanying miraculous transformations in the geography of Palestine to enable a river to flow down to the Dead Sea, are out of line with the New Testament's own interpretation, which relates the prophetic hope to its messianic fulfillment in Jesus... Indeed there

is a danger that obsession with apocalyptic scenarios involving literal reconstructions of Ezekiel's (and other Old Testament) visions may lead their devout adherents into precisely the kind of devaluing disregard for the complete, sufficient and final work of Christ that the letter to the Hebrews was written to warn against.[196]

Could it be that evangelical Christians have grown too used to hearing that the Old Testament prophecies must be applied in exactly the same way they applied in the days of Old Testament Israel? Could such emphasis have led to a neglect of the full significance of Christ's coming? New Testament scholar Timothy Paul Jones, professor at Southern Baptist Theological Seminary, suggests a better approach that is true to the New Testament's teaching about the transforming nature of Christ's ministry:

> The challenge is whether such a spiritual fulfillment really reflects what Ezekiel prophesied. The prophet saw a temple, not a group of people. If God fulfills this vision by dwelling among people, wouldn't that mean that God went back on his promises?
> Not necessarily!
> Think of it this way: Suppose a father in 1900 promised to give his young son a horse and buggy whenever his son married. During the son's later childhood and adolescence, this young man might have dreamt about the precise contours of the buggy and the breed of his horse. This was truly a good promise from his father! Now, suppose that, when the son married in the 1920s, the father did not give him a horse and buggy. Instead, the son and his bride received a brand-new automobile with leather seats, nickel-plated headlights, and battery ignition.
> Did the father break his promise to his son?
> Of course not. [Quoting G.K. Beale:] "The essence of the father's word has remained the same: a convenient mode of transportation. What has changed is the precise form of transportation." In the 1920s, new circumstances made the gift of a car far more appropriate than the finest horse and buggy. In the same way, on this side of the cross and empty tomb, perhaps a spiritual temple

represents a greater fulfillment of Ezekiel's words than the grandest physical structure.[197]

## Question #2: What about Romans 11?

Another question comes from the New Testament. If God's ultimate purpose for Israel is fulfilled in Christ, then what should be made of the promise about Israel's future in Romans 11?

> I do not want you to be ignorant of this mystery, brothers and sisters, so that you may not be conceited: Israel has experienced a hardening in part until the full number of the Gentiles has come in, and in this way all Israel will be saved. As it is written:
> "The deliverer will come from Zion;
> he will turn godlessness away from Jacob.
> And this is my covenant with them
> when I take away their sins."
> As far as the gospel is concerned, they are enemies for your sake; but as far as election is concerned, they are loved on account of the patriarchs, for God's gifts and his call are irrevocable. (Romans 11:25–29)

Some commentators have interpreted "Israel" in verse 26 as a reference to all of God's people, both Jews and Gentiles.[198] But the context of Romans 9 through 11 argues strongly against such an interpretation. "Israel" here refers to the Jewish people in distinction from the Gentiles or non-Jews.[199]

So what does "all Israel will be saved" mean? Does it refer to the turning of large numbers of Jews to their Messiah for salvation, or does it teach that Israel will be reestablished as a kingdom like it was in Old Testament times? Once again, context is crucial. Paul writes nothing in Romans 11 to indicate that he is thinking of the Jewish people as a geographical and political entity. Rather, Paul is deeply concerned throughout Romans 9 through 11 about their relationship to God through Jesus.

I speak the truth in Christ—I am not lying, my conscience confirms it through the Holy Spirit—I have great sorrow and unceasing anguish in my heart. For I could wish that I myself were cursed and cut off from Christ for the sake of my people, those of my own race, the people of Israel. (Romans 9:1–4a)

Brothers and sisters, my heart's desire and prayer to God for the Israelites is that they may be saved. For I can testify about them that they are zealous for God, but their zeal is not based on knowledge. Since they did not know the righteousness of God and sought to establish their own, they did not submit to God's righteousness. Christ is the culmination of the law so that there may be righteousness for everyone who believes. (Romans 10:1–4)

The prophecy of Romans 11:26 is an exciting one. Believers in Christ should look forward to the future turning of the Jewish people to their Messiah. But Romans 11 is not a political promise to modern Israel. From a Christian perspective, the issue of Israel as a nation is minimal compared to the hope of large numbers of Jews becoming followers of their Messiah.

## CONCLUSION

The misuse of Bible prophecy constitutes a monumental mistake on the part of evangelical Christians today. Reform needs to take place on many different levels. Christians need first to study the Old Testament prophets in historical context instead of immediately searching for tantalizing insights into possible future developments in the Middle East. Moreover, the prophets' call for repentance and justice needs to be heard and taken to heart, and that message needs to be applied to the modern nation of Israel. The injustices inflicted on the Palestinians by Israel's discriminatory policies call for repentance. As Amos wrote centuries ago, "Let justice roll on like a river, righteousness like a never-failing stream!"

## Chapter Eight
# Is This Replacement Theology?

*Reckless words pierce like a sword,
but the tongue of the wise brings healing.*

PROVERBS 12:18

A FEW MEN IN OUR CHURCH were discussing the interpretation of the Old Testament and the relationship between Israel and the church. After they listened to a brief summary of my viewpoint, two of them gave me looks of genuine concern and asked, "Do you believe in Replacement Theology?"

*Replacement Theology*—those two words have come to represent the seriously flawed theology of Christians who question the policies of the modern state of Israel. James Showers, executive director of The Friends of Israel, refers to this theological position as "The Black Sheep of Christendom."[200] John Hagee, the leader of Christians United for Israel castigates it as "an old heresy."[201] The executive director of Zion's Hope, Marvin Rosenthal, characterizes it as "dangerous and insidious."[202] The Bible, it is said, unquestionably teaches that Christians should support modern Israel. According to these critics, God says all that needs to be said in Genesis 12:3 when he promises Abraham and his descendants, "I will bless those who bless you, and whoever curses you I will curse." For Christians to withhold complete support for modern Israel can only mean that they have been deceived by a misinterpretation of what God teaches in his Word. That tragic deception is called supersessionism, or, as it is more commonly known, Replacement Theology.[203]

If only it were that simple. As soon as one tries to study Replacement Theology, a problem immediately emerges: "Replacement Theology" is a label that critics assign to a set of beliefs; it is not a title that people use to describe their own beliefs. That observation should introduce a strong note of caution to the discussion. What exactly *is* Replacement Theology? Have the critics fairly represented the beliefs they are so quick to attack? Who is teaching Replacement Theology today?

## What Is Replacement Theology?

Those who criticize Replacement Theology maintain that it includes five central elements that demand scrutiny:

1. God has permanently replaced or superseded ethnic Israel with "spiritual Israel" or the church.
2. The Old Testament is not interpreted in a literal or straightforward manner. Instead it is "spiritualized" or "allegorized."
3. There is no future for national Israel in the plan of God.
4. The church inherits the promises that God made to Old Testament Israel, and ethnic Israel receives all of the covenant curses.
5. Replacement Theology has led and will in all probability continue to lead to anti-Semitism.[204]

Each of these five elements needs to be examined. Do they accurately reflect the teaching of Christians who question and criticize the policies of modern Israel? Once again, we should be reminded that the Bible cautions against making a judgment before both sides of an issue have been heard.

## Replaced or Fulfilled?

Some theologians do use the word "replaced" in their statements about the relationship between Israel and the church,[205] but in recent years theologians have shied away from that terminology. "Fulfilled" has become the preferred term. Advocates speak now of Fulfillment Theology, not Replacement Theology.[206]

The change in names represents a more precise explanation of what is being stressed. The Bible does not teach a simple replacement of Israel by the church. As explained in previous chapters, the New Testament teaches that God's purposes for Israel have been fulfilled not primarily in the church but in Jesus Christ. Fulfillment Theologians stress that Jesus came to fulfill God's promise to Abraham in Genesis 12:3 that "all people on earth will be blessed through you."[207]

As a result of God's work through his Son, a new understanding of the covenant people of God emerges. In Romans 11 Paul uses the picture of an olive tree to describe the relationship between Israel and the church:

> If some of the branches have been broken off, and you, though a wild olive shoot, have been grafted in among the others and now share in the nourishing sap from the olive root, do not consider yourself to be superior to those other branches. If you do, consider this: You do not support the root, but the root supports you. You will say then, "Branches were broken off so that I could be grafted in." Granted. But they were broken off because of unbelief, and you stand by faith. Do not be arrogant, but tremble. For if God did not spare the natural branches, he will not spare you either. (Romans 11:17–21)

The olive tree represents the people of God. Some of its original Jewish branches have been broken off due to a lack of faith in Jesus the Messiah. Wild olive branches, representing Gentile believers, have been grafted onto the olive tree. In this illustration Paul does not teach that God has cut down the olive tree and planted another one in its place. That would be a genuine replacement of Israel with the church. Nor does Paul teach that God planted another olive tree next to the original one, as if God had one plan for the Jews and a different one for the Gentiles. Instead Paul teaches that God has grafted the Gentile believers onto the original Jewish tree so that there remains one tree which now includes Jews and Gentiles who have entrusted themselves to Jesus. The illustration emphasizes the continuity that exists between God's work in the Old Testament and the New Testament. Israel has not been replaced. Instead, the people of God have grown through Christ to include non-Jews who believe in the Jewish Messiah.[208]

## Literal or Spiritual?

Critics of Fulfillment Theology charge its adherents with spiritualizing or allegorizing the Bible in order to avoid its literal teaching. Ralph Dollinger summarizes the methodology of the theologians he disagrees with:

> More than providing additional and greater insight, the New Testament, they believe, is not only an interpreter of the meaning of Old Testament texts, *but it can reinterpret them.* More specifically, physical promises made to Israel by Old Testament Prophets, they believe, are often reinterpreted by New Testament writers to have a *spiritual* fulfillment in the Church. Accordingly, actual Old Testament predictions pertaining to Israel's future, physical restoration are discounted.[209]

This charge is based on a simple misunderstanding. It confuses interpretation and application. The Old Testament should first be interpreted in terms of what the original recipients would have understood its words to have meant. But now that Jesus Christ has come and completed God's revelation of himself, there is a new application of that teaching.[210]

In Genesis 12:3, God says "I will bless those who bless you, and whoever curses you I will curse; and all people on earth will be blessed through you." The interpretation of that promise is not up for question. God was referring to Abraham's biological descendants. In its Old Testament setting, the teaching applied directly to the nation of Israel because Israel was the focus of God's attention and action. But with the coming of Christ, the application—*not* the interpretation—of Genesis 12:3 changes. As Galatians 3:7–9 teaches, the promise made to Abraham has been fulfilled in Christ. It is through him that all people on earth will be blessed. Therefore, the application of Genesis 12:3 should be understood to apply to Jesus. Those who bless him will be blessed and those who curse him will be cursed.

## Future or Finished?

Is God finished with the Jews? Critics maintain that Replacement Theology teaches that God has no plan for Abraham's descendants. James Showers

## Is This Replacement Theology?

writes, "Replacement Theology teaches there is no future for national Israel: God has thoroughly rejected Israel and no longer has a place for it in His plan for eternity apart from the salvation of individual Jewish people."[211]

But does that description accurately depict the teaching of contemporary theologians who believe that the promises made to Israel in the Old Testament have been fulfilled in Christ? In his sermon on "The Place of Israel," the highly respected Christian preacher and leader John Stott rejects the idea that God has no future plan for Israel:

> If "Israel" meant descendants of Jacob in the Old Testament and means believers in Jesus in the New Testament, must we conclude that God has no special future for physical Israel? That was the very question which Paul's teaching prompted Jewish objectors to ask. "Did God reject his people" (Romans 11:1). Moreover, two answers are given to the question each beginning with the emphatic negative "by no means!", "Not at all!" or "God forbid!" (Romans 11:1, 11)

Stott goes on to consider the teaching of Romans 11:24–26b and concludes, "the hardening of Israel is only temporary. Later, Paul seems to be saying, there will be a widespread turning of Jews to Christ."[212]

Stott's understanding of Paul's teaching in Romans 11 is not unique. In fact, his belief that God has a plan for the future of the Jewish people represents a view that is widely accepted and taught today.[213] Craig Blaising summarizes:

> ...after the awful tragedy of the Holocaust, many Biblical scholars have reassessed the anti-Jewish bias by which Scripture has been read, with the consequences being a major shift of opinion on the New Testament expectation of a future for Israel. Key to this has been the development of a consensus regarding Paul's teaching in Romans 9–11 that there is indeed a future in the plan of God for Israel—not a redefined Israel, but ethnic-national Israel.[214]

God is not finished with Israel! In his providential will, God is working through all nations of the world to fulfill his purposes. That, of course, includes the modern nation of Israel. Furthermore, Romans 11 teaches that God is presently using the Jewish majority's rejection of Christ to spread the good news of salvation in Christ to the non-Jewish world. At a future time the majority of Jews will come to faith in their Messiah, and their trust in him will then usher in the fullness of God's plan.

## Promises or Curses?

Critics accuse Fulfillment Theology of teaching that the church inherits the promises that God made to Old Testament Israel while ethnic Israel receives all of the covenant curses. That idea may appear to be a logical deduction from the church's "replacement" of Israel in God's plan, but evidence that Fulfillment Theologians actually teach that idea today is difficult to find.

Furthermore, the previous section demonstrated that contemporary Fulfillment Theologians do believe that the New Testament promises a future for ethnic Israel. Romans 11:25 looks forward to a time when large numbers of Jews will enjoy the full salvation that God has brought to earth through his Son. What greater future could there be than to know Christ as Savior and to glorify God in one's daily life on earth before entering into the eternal rest accomplished by Christ to the glory of his Father?

## Anti-Semitic—or Guilt by Association?

Of all the charges leveled against Fulfillment Theology, the most serious one is that it has led and will continue to lead to anti-Semitism. The critics give the impression that this outcome is almost inevitable.

> In most places where it held sway, replacement theology led inexorably to anti-Semitic opinion, legislation and action. Rejected by God, the Jews found little mercy from man.[215]

> Replacement Theology has been the "black sheep" of Christendom because, over the past 2,000 years, it has led to countless acts of anti-Semitism by some in the church—and I cannot overemphasize the word *countless*.[216]

## Is This Replacement Theology?

> Historically, it has been difficult for those in the church to subscribe to Replacement Theology and avoid anti-Semitism.[217]

> The error of Replacement Theology is like a cancer in the Church that has not only caused it to violate God's Word concerning the Jewish people and Israel, but it made us into instruments of hate, not love in God's Name.[218]

> Wherever replacement theology has flourished, the Jews have had to run for cover.[219]

Those are serious charges. If true, then Replacement or Fulfillment Theology should be categorically rejected and repudiated. But are they true?

First, it must be recognized that over the last two thousand years Christianity has at times been unmistakably anti-Semitic. Hatred for the Jews has not been advocated by minor or fringe figures within the church but by major leaders.

In AD 387, the passionate reformer and eloquent preacher John Chrysostom preached a series of eight anti-Jewish sermons in Antioch.

> The Jews are the most worthless of all men—they are lecherous, greedy, rapacious—they are perfidious murderers of Christians, they worship the devil, their religion is a sickness…
>
> The Jews are the odious assassins of Christ and for killing God there is no expiation possible, no indulgence or pardon. Christians may never cease vengeance, and the Jews must live in servitude for ever. God always hated the Jews, and whoever has intercourse with Jews will be rejected on Judgment Day. It is incumbent upon all Christians to hate the Jews.[220]

Such fiery rhetoric was followed by violent pogroms against Jews in Antioch in the early fifth century. The synagogues of the city were destroyed, and charges of ritual murder were leveled against the Jews. Eventually they were expelled from the city.[221]

Over the centuries the Roman Catholic Church formalized its rejection and oppression of the Jews.

| Date | Synod or Council | Canonical Law |
|------|------------------|---------------|
| 306 | Synod of Elvira | Prohibition of intermarriage and of sexual intercourse between Christians and Jews. Jews and Christians not permitted to eat together. |
| 535 | Synod of Clermont | Jews not allowed to hold public office. |
| 538 | 3rd Synod of Orleans | Jews not allowed to employ Christian servants or possess Christian slaves. Jews not permitted to show themselves in the streets during Passion Week. |
| 681 | 12th Synod of Toledo | Burning of the Talmud and other books. |
| 1078 | Synod of Gerona | Jews obliged to pay taxes for support of the Church to the same extent as Christians. |
| 1215 | 4th Lateran Council | The marking of Jewish clothes with a badge. |
| 1222 | Council of Oxford | Construction of new synagogues prohibited. |
| 1267 | Cynod of Breslau | Compulsory ghettos. |
| 1279 | Synod of Ofen | Christians not permitted to sell or rent real estate to Jews. |
| 1434 | Council of Basel | Jews not permitted to act as agents in the conclusion of contracts between Christians, especially marriage contracts. Jews not permitted to obtain academic degrees. |

222

Anti-Semitism was not limited to Roman Catholicism. The famous Protestant Reformer Martin Luther wrote in Section 11 of *The Jews and Their Lies*:

> First, their synagogues or churches should be set on fire, and whatever does not burn up should be covered or spread over with dirt so that no one may ever be able to see a cinder or stone of it. And this ought to be done for the honor of God and of Christianity in order that God may see that we are Christians.... Secondly, their homes should be broken down and destroyed. Thirdly, they should be deprived of their prayer books and Talmuds in which such idolatry, lies, cursing and blasphemy are taught.
>
> Fourthly, their Rabbis must be forbidden under threat of death to teach any more.... Fifthly, passport and traveling privileges should be absolutely forbidden the Jews. Let them stay at home. Sixthly, they ought to be stopped from usury. For this reason, as said before, everything they possess they stole and robbed from us

through their usury, for they have no other means of support. Seventhly, let the young and strong Jews and Jewesses be given the flail, the ax, the hose, the spade, the distaff, and spindle, and let them earn their bread by the sweat of their noses....

If, however, we are afraid that they might harm us personally, or our wives, children, servants, cattle, etc., then...let us drive them out of the country for all time.[223]

The tragic and sinful reality of anti-Semitism in the history of the Christian faith must be acknowledged, but an investigation of the subject must not stop there. While famous Christians like John Chrysostom and Martin Luther were outspoken in their vehemence against the Jews, the past should not be automatically equated with the present. Anti-Semitism can be found among fringe groups that claim some connection to Christianity, but are Christian theologians—in particular Fulfillment Theologians—today following Chrysostom's and Luther's example, or is this an example of guilt by association?

Evangelical theologians today grieve past practices of anti-Semitism. For example, John Stott condemns and renounces anti-Semitism:

Away then with anti-Semitism! It has been an appalling scandal in the history of Europe and even the Christian church has been implicated. Christians should be "pro-Semitic," in the sense that we recognize how the people of Israel have been highly favoured by God. We Gentiles are their debtors, Paul wrote (Romans 15:27). We owe them a huge spiritual debt, especially in their bequest to the world of both the Scriptures and the Christ.[224]

In addition, it should be recognized that the accusation of anti-Semitism has been leveled against Christians who take a variety of approaches toward the modern state of Israel. It is not a charge limited to those whose theology has been labeled as Replacement or Fulfillment Theology. Christian Zionists who follow a dispensational interpretation of the Bible have also been suspected of being anti-Semitic.[225] For example, one Orthodox Jewish journalist, Gershom Gorenberg, expresses hesitancy about the love for Jews espoused by Christian Zionists who are infatuated with Bible prophecy:

> The potential for anti-Semitism is clear today—precisely because the dispensationalism accepted by millions assigns Jews such a large part in the drama. As long as believers expect the End tomorrow, the result is love for Jews. Yet that love is akin to what a fan feels while stalking a movie star, unable to distinguish between the actress and the part she once played in a movie. When the "terminal" generation refuses to reach its terminus, an old frustration with Jews who won't play their role is all too likely to surface.[226]

Charges of anti-Semitism extend beyond Replacement Theology or even Christian Zionism. The New Testament and Christianity as a whole have been accused of being inherently anti-Semitic. In the summer of 2012 the Bible Society of Israel sent the members of the Israeli Knesset copies of a newly published version of the New Testament. One Knesset member, Michael Ben-Ari, tore it up and threw it in a trash can. He explained, "This abhorrent book promoted the murders of millions of Jews during the Inquisition and the *autos da fé* [burning of heretics]…this is an ugly missionary provocation by the Church, there's no doubt that the book and its senders belong in the trash of history."[227] To Ben-Ari the threat comes not from one particular school of Christian theology but from the New Testament itself.

With the issue of anti-Semitism, two warnings must be simultaneously considered. To ignore either is to invite misunderstanding and tragedy. David Brog, who is Jewish yet worked as the Executive Director of Christians United for Israel from 2006 to 2015, explains both warnings in his book, *Standing with Israel*:

> Anti-Semitism proved itself to be the most deadly hatred of the 20th century. The record from prior centuries only confirms the danger. The charge of anti-Semitism, therefore, remains a charge of enormous severity. It is a point of view for which no excuse can be made.…
>
> Jews have learned through bitter experience never to ignore possible signs of anti-Semitism. Those who dismissed Hitler's anti-

## Is This Replacement Theology?

Semitism as meaningless talk likely perished in his gas chambers....

Yet while maintaining this heightened vigilance, the Jewish community must also maintain its common sense and decency. If the charge of anti-Semitism is to retain its enormous power, then it must not be leveled frivolously. Distinctions must be made between this hatred so grave and lesser crimes of insensitivity or ignorance. All suspect comments must be taken seriously. But conclusions must be reached, not jumped to.[228]

Brog's second point applies not just to the Jewish community but to the Christian community as well. Today it is necessary to be on guard not just against anti-Semitism but also against frivolous charges of anti-Semitism. Such accusations come with enormous force. To suggest that someone might be anti-Semitic can be enough to intimidate that person into silence. Merely to be accused of anti-Semitism can ruin a person's reputation. Christian writers and speakers must guard against smearing other believers in Christ with such forceful denunciations unless they have solid evidence for the accusation.

Furthermore, it needs to be recognized that supersessionism or Replacement Theology can take different forms. *Punitive supersessionism* justifies oppression and persecution of the Jews on the grounds that God has rejected the Jews forever. That form must be distinguished from *theological supersessionism*, which maintains that God's purposes for Israel have found their ultimate and complete expression in Jesus Christ.[229]

Popular literature on this subject rarely recognizes the distinction. David Brog provides a welcome exception to that trend:

> There remain millions of Protestants in America, many of whom are in fact evangelicals, who have not renounced replacement theology. On the contrary, these Protestants fervently embrace a form of replacement theology that they refer to by the more positive name of "covenant theology"...in the absence of Christian faith, the Jewish people and the modern State of Israel enjoy no special theological status. This view is not anti-Semitic, and those who adhere to it are not anti-Semites. Rather, it is my thesis that replacement theology creates the *potential* for anti-Semitism in the church. Human

nature being what it is, this potential for anti-Semitism has in the past been fully realized. In America today, many who embrace covenant theology recognize this potential, and they are committed to opposing anti-Semitism in their churches.[230]

Brog's careful distinction is noteworthy because it is so rarely stated.[231] Unfortunately Brog explains it not in the body of his book but only in an endnote.

Christians today need to be on guard against anti-Semitism. As John Stott said, "Away then with anti-Semitism!" We also need to be extremely careful about accusing other believers in Christ of anti-Semitism. In today's world such a powerful accusation may be immediately embraced by others and result in the ruin of someone's reputation. Away then with false accusations of anti-Semitism!

## CAUTION!

Proverbs 12:18 provides a wise reminder: "Reckless words pierce like a sword, but the tongue of the wise brings healing." Words are powerful, and they need to be used with care. Christians have a duty before God to make sure they do not repeat the grievous sins of the past and fall into the sin of anti-Semitism. Christians must also guard against falsely accusing other believers in Christ of being anti-Semitic. It is irresponsible to describe as anti-Semitic every contemporary Christian theologian who believes that God's purposes for Old Testament Israel have been fulfilled in Jesus Christ. It is unjust to suggest that every criticism of modern Israel's policies arises solely from anti-Semitism.

Therefore, it should be stated without apology:

- It is *not* anti-Semitic to criticize Israel's discrimination against Palestinian citizens of Israel.
- It is *not* anti-Semitic to criticize Israel's occupation of the West Bank.
- It is *not* anti-Semitic to criticize Israel's construction of the Separation Barrier.
- It is *not* anti-Semitic to criticize Israel's harassment of Palestinians at checkpoints.

- It is *not* anti-Semitic to criticize Israel's settlements in the West Bank.
- It is *not* anti-Semitic to criticize Israel's restriction on Palestinians' access to water.
- It is *not* anti-Semitic to criticize Israel's complacency over settler violence.
- It is *not* anti-Semitic to criticize Israel's practice of administrative detention.
- It is *not* anti-Semitic to criticize Israel's practice of home demolition.
- It is *not* anti-Semitic to criticize Israel's virtual imprisonment of Gaza.

As the first two sections of this book have demonstrated, American evangelicals need to move beyond snap historical, political, and theological judgments. All of the complexities of the Israeli-Palestinian conflict require careful investigation. The role of the United States needs now to be considered. Is it an honest broker between the two sides? What should the United States be doing to bring peace and justice to Palestine and Israel? Should American evangelicals be calling for a change in their country's foreign policy?

# Part 3
# Evangelicals and Injustice

## Chapter Nine
# A Plea for Tough Love

*Rescue those being led away to death;*
*hold back those staggering toward slaughter.*
*If you say, "But we knew nothing about this,"*
*does not he who weighs the heart perceive it?*
*Does not he who guards your life know it?*
*Will he not repay everyone according to what they have done?*

Proverbs 24:11–12

AFTER TALKING ABOUT PALESTINE AND ISRAEL one Sunday evening at our church, a woman came up to me and commented, "I learned a lot in what you said tonight, but it seemed to me that your presentation was not balanced. It was terribly one-sided." That single observation made me do a lot of thinking. Was my presentation out of balance? Had I been too harsh on Israel and not critical enough of Palestinians and Arab nations?

Impartiality is important. Romans 3:23 can describe nations as well as individuals: "For all have sinned and fall short of the glory of God." Neither the Israelis nor the Palestinians have always acted justly. Americans should hear both the Israeli narrative and the Palestinian narrative.

But questions about balance work both ways. How many times do Christians hear sermons or read literature calling for support for modern Israel and then ask, "Is this balanced? Why are we not being told about the Nakba and the suffering of the Palestinians?" It appears that the question of balance is only raised when it is Israel being criticized.

Striving for balance is good. Hearing both sides of an issue is necessary and wise. But straddling the fence and taking a middle-of-the-road approach can be an excuse for complacency and refusing to take a stand. When persistent policies of injustice are exposed, calls for repentance need to be issued.

It is good that Christians love Israel, but genuine love cannot be reduced to simply approving what any person or nation does.

> Better is open rebuke
> > than hidden love.
> Wounds from a friend can be trusted,
> > But an enemy multiplies kisses.
>
> PROVERBS 27:5-6

> Whoever rebukes a person will in the end gain favor
> > rather than one who has a flattering tongue.
>
> PROVERBS 28:23

Love must be grounded in the truth and ready to speak that truth even when it will not be readily embraced. It requires courage and a willingness to accept rejection. Perhaps it is time for the United States to practice such tough love in its relationship with modern Israel.

## AMERICAN FOREIGN POLICY

Israeli leaders present their people as a tiny nation of victims surrounded by hateful countries bent on their destruction.[232] They fail to mention that Israel is currently ranked as the eleventh most powerful military in the world in its conventional war-making capabilities.[233] It ranks higher than any of its Middle Eastern neighbors, and that ranking does not take nuclear weapons into consideration. Israel does not publicly acknowledge that it possesses nuclear weapons, but it is widely known that it is the only country in the Middle East that has them. The Institute for Middle East Understanding summarizes Israel's military potential:

> Israel's military is one of the most advanced and powerful forces in the world. Its conventional weaponry, much of it purchased from

the United States or produced by the highly developed Israeli arms industry, includes nearly 600 combat airplanes, 200 attack helicopters, 3,600 tanks, over 9,000 armored personnel carriers, and 360 ballistic missiles.

Its navy operates three Dolphin-class submarines believed capable of launching nuclear warheads. With an estimated 200–300 such warheads, Israel is considered the sixth-ranked nuclear power in the world and capable of delivering nuclear warheads by missile or from aircraft. It is also suspected of holding stocks of chemical and biological weapons.[234]

The emphasis placed on Israel's vulnerability is described by Avraham Burg, former speaker of the Knesset, as "exaggerated securitism." He explains, "Our state is well established and powerful, almost without precedence…we try to hide this splendor by constantly whining."[235] Former Israeli Foreign Minister Shlomo Ben-Ami admits that since 1948, security has been elevated to the status of a "sacred cow." Israel, he acknowledges, has a "penchant for formulating policies only on the basis of worst-case scenarios."[236]

Americans should also be aware of the unique position that Israel enjoys when it comes to American foreign policy. A letter that President Gerald Ford sent to Prime Minister Yitzhak Rabin on September 1, 1975 demonstrates the attitude of the United States toward Israel that has been followed for the last four decades: "Should the U.S. desire in the future to put forward proposals of its own, it will make every effort to coordinate with Israel its proposals with a view to refraining from putting forth proposals that Israel would consider unsatisfactory."[237] In 2011 Vice-President Joe Biden put it more bluntly: "When it comes to Israel's security there can be no daylight—no daylight—between Israel and the U.S."[238] In other words, the United States will not publicly oppose what the Israeli government wants. Israel, in effect, has veto power over any suggestion the United States might consider making.

Israel annually receives $3.1 billion in Foreign Military Finance from the United States. Furthermore, Israel currently enjoys privileges that other countries do not receive. For example, the Foreign Military Finance program usually requires recipient countries to spend their aid money in the United States, but Congress grants Israel a special exemption from that requirement. Israel is allowed to spend one out of every four US military aid dollars on its own defense industry. Furthermore, Israel receives its aid according to a unique schedule, as explained by John Mearsheimer and Stephen Walt in *The Israel Lobby*:

> Most recipients of American foreign aid get their money in quarterly installments, but since 1982, the annual foreign aid bill has included a special clause specifying that Israel is to receive its entire annual appropriation in the first thirty days of the fiscal year. This is akin to receiving your entire annual salary on January 1 and thus being able to earn interest on the unspent portion until you used it.

Mearsheimer and Walt point out that Israel also benefits from additional privileges that no other country enjoys.

> Remarkably, Israel is the only recipient of U.S. economic aid that does not have to account for how it is spent.... This exemption makes it virtually impossible for the United States to prevent its subsidies from being used for purposes that it opposes, such as building settlements on the West Bank.[239]

The June 2015 Congressional Research Service's report "U.S. Foreign Aid to Israel" summarizes the relationship between Israel and the United States:

> Israel is the largest cumulative recipient of U.S. foreign assistance since World War II. To date, the United States has provided Israel $124.3 billion (current, or non-inflation-adjusted, dollars) in bilateral assistance. Almost all U.S. bilateral aid to Israel is in the form of military assistance, although in the past Israel also received significant economic assistance. Strong congressional support for Israel has resulted in Israel receiving benefits not available to any other countries....[240]

## A Plea for Tough Love

The difference between the way the United States treats the Palestinian Authority and the way it deals with Israel is stark. From the time that limited Palestinian self-rule was established in the West Bank and Gaza in the mid-1990s, the United States has committed approximately $5 billion in assistance to the Palestinians. In 2012, the Palestinians asked for and received United Nations recognition as a "non-member state." What was the response of the United States? Due to congressional holds, the disbursement of their aid was delayed. Those holds were eventually released, but Congress then enacted legislation to restrict aid to the Palestinian authority.

> Palestinian Membership in the United Nations or U.N. Specialized Agencies, and Action at the International Criminal Court (ICC): No Economic Support Fund aid is permitted to the PA if the Palestinians:
> 1. obtain from this point forward (the restriction does not apply to Palestinian membership in UNESCO) "the same standing as member states or full membership as a state in the United Nations or any specialized agency thereof outside an agreement negotiated between Israel and the Palestinians"; or
> 2. initiate "an International Criminal Court judicially authorized investigation, or actively support such an investigation, that subjects Israeli nationals to an investigation for alleged crimes against Palestinians."[241]

In 2014 the Palestinians did sign fifteen multilateral treaties and conventions. That move opened the possibility that they could request an International Criminal Court investigation of Israel's actions in Gaza and the West Bank. Once again the Palestinians were warned that they would lose US aid if they dared to file a lawsuit against Israel.[242]

How does the United States treat Israel, which receives $3.1 billion in Foreign Military Finance every year? In the last forty-eight years, over 500,000 Israelis have moved into settlements in the Occupied Palestinian Territories in defiance of international law. During that same period the United States has objected to those settlements, referring to them as "illegal," "unnecessarily provocative," and "an obstacle to peace."[243] The breakdown of the negotiations led by Secretary of State John Kerry in 2013 and 2014 was attributed to decisions and actions of both Palestinians and Israelis, but US negotiators pointed specifically to Israel's refusal to budge on the issue of settlements.

> The issue of Israeli settlements humiliated the Palestinian negotiators and poisoned the talks, according to statements by U.S. negotiators. When Israel announced 700 new settlement apartments in early April, before the April 29 deadline for the talks, "Poof, that was sort of the moment," Kerry told a Senate panel. Warned Indyk [U.S. Special Envoy for Israeli-Palestinian Negotiations] at a gathering of the Washington Institute for Near East Policy, "Rampant settlement activity—especially in the midst of negotiations—doesn't just undermine Palestinian trust in the purpose of the negotiations; it can undermine Israel's Jewish future."[244]

Did any members of Congress push for a reduction in US foreign aid to Israel due to its intransigence? No. Israel's refusal to stop the settlements has not cost Israel any funding from America.

Can such preferential treatment of Israel be characterized as just? Why does the United States treat Israel so gently when they have consistently violated international law for the last forty-eight years? Why is the provision of a seat for the Palestinians as a "non-member state" at the United Nations such a grave threat to the security of Israel? Why is an investigation by the International Criminal Court so dangerous to Israel's existence? Is it even conceivable to describe the treatment that the United States gives to Palestine and Israel as being based on principles of justice?

## ZIONISM TODAY

In American politics today, support for the modern nation of Israel can be characterized as *unquestioned, uncritical,* and *unconditional.* Americans are told that they should be pro-Israel because of the suffering of the Jews throughout history—particularly during the Holocaust—and because Israel is the only democratic nation in the Middle East. Some protests against America's foreign policy do take place, but the US's support for Israel remains virtually unchanged. For American politicians to question Israel's policies, much less criticize them, is to commit political suicide. To suggest that support for Israel should not be unconditional but subject to the same kind of oversight that other countries receive is to run the risk of being charged with anti-Semitism.

In July 2014, both the United States Senate and House of Representatives passed resolutions condemning Hamas for firing rockets into Israel. Neither resolution included one word of criticism or even acknowledgement of Israel's blockade of Gaza, which resulted in food insecurity, high unemployment, lack of potable water, and power outages. Furthermore, both of the congressional resolutions passed unanimously. The 113th Congress was infamous for its inability to come together on almost any issue, yet it supported Israel's policies in regard to Gaza without one vote of dissent.[245]

An exchange of opinions that took place in October of 2012 demonstrates what happens when the unquestioned, uncritical, and unconditional support for Israel is challenged. A group of fifteen Christian organizations sent an open letter to Congress:

> As Christian leaders in the United States, it is our moral responsibility to question the continuation of unconditional U.S. financial assistance to the government of Israel. Realizing a just and lasting peace will require this accountability, as continued U.S. military assistance to Israel—offered without conditions or accountability—will only serve to sustain the status quo and Israel's military occupation of the Palestinian territories.[246]

After the publication of that open letter, Rabbi Steve Gutow, president of the Jewish Council of Public Affairs, responded:

> The participation of these leaders in yet another one-sided anti-Israel campaign cannot be viewed apart from the vicious anti-Zionism that has gone virtually unchecked in several of these denominations. We remain committed to the enterprise of interfaith relations because it is central to the development of a just and righteous society. But these churches have squandered our trust.[247]

This exchange is astounding. The letter from the Christian organizations specifically asked for an examination of the "unconditional U.S. financial assistance." It did not call for the elimination of foreign aid to Israel but only that there be some degree of accountability for the way that Israel spends US taxpayers' dollars. Is asking Congress to examine how US foreign aid is spent by Israel really "one-sided" and "anti-Israel"? Doesn't Congress regularly convene hearings to look into how our country's money is used? Is a call for congressional oversight of foreign aid to Israel really an example of "vicious anti-Semitism"?

## ZIONISM QUESTIONED AND CRITIQUED

Most Americans are unaware that many Israelis are critical of their nation's policies toward Palestinians living in the West Bank and Gaza. The media regularly report on what Prime Minister Netanyahu says in defense of Israel's policies, but rarely do they report on the numerous criticisms penned by Israeli citizens and American Jews.

B'Tselem, the Israeli Information Center for Human Rights in the Occupied Territories, "was established in February 1989 by a group of prominent academics, attorneys, journalists, and Knesset members. It endeavors to document and educate the Israeli public and policy makers about human rights violations in the Occupied Territories, combat the phenomenon of denial prevalent among the Israeli public, and help create a human rights culture in Israel."[248] B'Tselem produces carefully researched and detailed reports on human rights violations by both Israelis and Palestinians.

In January 2002, fifty-one soldiers signed The Combatant Letter, which stated, "We shall not continue to fight beyond the 1967 borders in order to dominate, expel, starve and humiliate an entire people."[249] On September 24, 2003, The Pilots' Letter was signed by twenty-seven reserve and active duty Israeli pilots. They wrote:

> We, for whom the Israel Defense Forces and the Air Force are an inalienable part of ourselves, refuse to continue to harm innocent civilians.
>
> These actions are illegal and immoral, and are a direct result

of the ongoing occupation which is corrupting the Israeli society. Perpetuation of the occupation is fatally harming the security of the state of Israel and its moral strength.[250]

The Commandos' Letter followed in December 2003. Thirteen members of one of the Israeli Defense Force's most prestigious combat units wrote Prime Minister Sharon:

- We shall no longer lend a hand in the occupation of the territories
- We shall no longer take part in the deprivation of basic human rights from millions of Palestinians
- We shall no longer serve as a shield in the crusade of the settlements
- We shall no longer corrupt our moral character in missions of oppression
- We shall no longer deny our responsibility as soldiers of the Israeli DEFENSE force.[251]

In June of 2004, the Olga Document was composed by Israeli scholars and activists and then signed by over two hundred professors and artists. It described Israel as being "up to its neck in the mire of occupation and oppression while it goes on extending the settlements."

> We are united in a critique of Zionism, based as it is on refusal to acknowledge the indigenous people of this country and on denial of their rights, on dispossession of their lands, and on adoption of separation as a fundamental principle and way of life. Adding insult to injury, Israel persists in its refusal to bear any responsibility for its deeds, from the expulsion of the majority of Palestinians from their homeland more than half a century ago, to the present erection of ghetto walls around the remaining Palestinians in the towns and villages of the West Bank.[252]

An organization called Breaking the Silence was created by veterans of the Israeli Defense Force in 2004 to "expose the Israeli public to the reality of everyday life in the Occupied Territories. We endeavor to stimulate public debate about the price paid for a reality in which young soldiers face a civilian population on a daily basis, and are engaged in the control of that population's everyday life."[253]

Avi Shlaim grew up in Israel and served in the Israeli Defense Force in the mid-1960s. He is now professor emeritus of international relations at the University of Oxford. In *The Iron Wall*, he provides a detailed history of Israel's policy toward its Arab neighbors from 1948 to 2006. In the epilogue of the book he provided his conclusion:

> Since 1967 Israel has tried every conceivable method of ending the conflict with the Palestinians except the obvious one—ending the occupation. The occupation has inflicted indescribable suffering on the Palestinians, but it has also had a corrosive effect on Israel itself, turning it into a brutal colonial power, curtailing civil liberties at home, and eroding the foundations of its democracy. Military occupation has inescapable consequences: it brutalizes and dehumanizes the colonizer, it embitters the colonized, and it breeds racism. Denying freedom to the 1.7 million inhabitants of Gaza and the 2.6 million of the West Bank is undemocratic, unjust, unethical, and unsustainable.[254]

Born in Israel, Ahron Bergman was a soldier in the 1982 Lebanon War. He now teaches at the Department of War Studies, King's College London. *Cursed Victory*, published in 2014, records the history of Israel and the occupied territories since 1967. In the final paragraph of the book, he concluded:

> I believe that the verdict of history will regard the four decades of occupation described in this book as a black mark in Israeli and, indeed, Jewish history. This was a period in which Israel, helped by the Jewish diaspora, particularly in America, proved that even nations which have suffered unspeakable tragedies of their own can

act in similarly cruel ways when in power themselves. Back in 1967, the defence minister at the time, Moshe Dayan, observed that if he had to choose to be occupied by any force from among the nations of the world, he doubted he would choose Israel. He was right; looking back it is clear that Israel was—and in the time of writing is still—a heavy-handed and brutal occupier.[255]

In 2011, Moshe Dayan's widow Ruth expressed her disgust with Israel's present policies. "And this continuous expansion of the settlements everywhere—I cannot accept it. I cannot tolerate this deterioration in the territories and the roadblocks everywhere. And that horrible wall! It's not right."[256]

Miko Peled's grandfather was a signer of Israel's Declaration of Independence, and his father was Matti Peled, a respected Israeli general in the 1967 War. In 1997, Miko's thirteen-year-old niece was killed by a suicide bomber. That murder started Peled on a journey to understand the conflict in his homeland. To his surprise, he learned that what he had been taught as a young Israeli was not the full truth. *The General's Son* tells the story of his transformation from a devoted Zionist to a peace activist.

*My Promised Land* is Israeli journalist Ari Shavit's candid examination of the complex internal and external challenges currently facing his nation.

> The State of Israel refuses to see its Arab citizens. It has not yet found a way to integrate properly one-fifth of its population. The Arabs who were not driven away in 1948 have been oppressed by Zionism for decades. The Jewish state confiscated much of their land, trampled many of their rights, and did not accord them real equality. In recent years, oppression lessened, but it was not replaced by a genuine civil covenant that will give Arab Israelis their full rights.[257]

Perhaps the former speaker of the Israeli Knesset, Avraham Burg, best summarized the opinion of a growing number of Israelis when he wrote, "We are not as bad as we are depicted by our critics, but we are not as good as we describe ourselves."[258]

American Jews have also voiced their criticism of modern Israel's policies. On May 18, 2011, the American Jewish organization called J Street, which describes itself as pro-Israel and pro-peace, ran an ad in Israeli newspapers:

> We, the undersigned, therefore call upon any person seeking peace and liberty and upon all nations to join us in welcoming the Palestinian Declaration of Independence, and to support the efforts of the citizens of the two states to maintain peaceful relations on the basis of secure borders and good neighborliness. The end of the occupation is a fundamental condition for the liberation of the two peoples, the realization of the Israeli Declaration of Independence and a future of peaceful coexistence.[259]

Rabbi Michael Lerner wrote *Embracing Israel/Palestine*, an informative and remarkably balanced book that presents both the Palestinian and Israeli narratives. "We need to learn how two groups of human beings, each containing the usual range of people—from loving to hateful, rational to demented, idealistic to self-centered—could end up feeling so angry at each other."[260]

In *Wrestling in the Daylight,* another rabbi, Brant Rosen, described his long struggle with defending Zionism. After Israel assaulted Gaza in December 2008, Rosen wrote, "I realized how utterly tired I had become. Tired of trying to excuse the inexcusable. Tired of using torturous, exhausting rationalizations to explain away what I really knew in my heart was sheer and simple *oppression*."[261]

In *Genesis*, John B. Judis traced the history of President Truman's recognition of Israel in 1948, and he concluded his book with observations about the current state of the Israeli-Palestinian conflict.

> Israelis and their supporters spent decades trying to explain away the dark side of their conquest of Palestine… But the Palestinian people have not gone away and have grown in number, and are a living reminder that what was a triumph for Zionism in 1948 has been an enduring catastrophe for them.…
>
> The main lesson of this narrative is that whatever wrongs were

done to the Jews of Europe and later to those of the Arab Middle East and North Africa—and there were great wrongs inflicted—the Zionists who came to Palestine to establish a state trampled on the rights of the Arabs who already lived there. That wrong has never been adequately addressed....

If America has tilted in the past toward Zionism and toward Israel, it is now time to redress that moral balance.[262]

## CHRISTIAN ZIONISM TODAY

Christian Zionism, like Zionism in general, calls not just for support of Israel but for support that is *unquestioning, uncritical,* and *unconditional.* Christian Zionism, however, adds a theological rationale to the humanitarian and political reasons for supporting Israel.

Outspoken expressions of Christian Zionism are found in organizations like the International Christian Embassy in Jerusalem and John Hagee's Christians United for Israel. In November of 2010 the latter group produced "The Israel Pledge":

> We believe that the Jewish people have a right to live in their ancient land of Israel, and that the modern State of Israel is the fulfillment of this historic right.
>
> We maintain that there is no excuse for acts of terrorism against Israel and that Israel has the same right as every other nation to defend her citizens from such violent attacks.
>
> We pledge to stand with our brothers and sisters in Israel and to speak out on their behalf whenever and wherever necessary until the attacks stop and they are finally living in peace and security with their neighbors.[263]

Christian writers provide a steady stream of literature supporting Israel. Citing Genesis 12:3 and selected verses from the Old Testament prophets, they argue that God is unconditionally on Israel's side. Tim LaHaye's *Left Behind* novels strongly suggest the same. Joel Rosenberg writes both fiction and nonfiction in support of Christian Zionism.

Some theologians do acknowledge that modern Israel has done things that are wrong. Their verbal support for Israel cannot be described as unquestioning or uncritical, but their criticisms are neither specific nor emphasized. For example, theologian John Feinberg says, "In the current struggle between Israelis and Palestinians, there is plenty of blame to be shared by all sides in this struggle. Nothing about dispensationalism, or any other form of evangelical Christian theology, requires supporting acts of sin done by anyone."[264] Another theologian, Wayne Grudem, states, "For several reasons, therefore, it seems to me that the United States should count Israel as a close ally and, while not supporting Israel when it does wrong, should still give special favor and protection to that nation."[265]

Such acknowledgements of Israel's wrongdoing are rarely found among Christian Zionists.[266] When they do appear, they unfortunately produce little impact because they are so general. Grudem, for example, expresses concern for inadequate protection of religious freedom within Israel, but he does not call for Israel to change its practices or for the United States to challenge Israel's policies.[267] Such criticism amounts to nothing more than an observation. It has no practical impact. In effect, the support of Christian Zionists for Israel's policies remains unconditional.

## Christian Zionism Questioned and Critiqued

Because it is so pervasive, Christian Zionism is best described as a populist movement.[268] In fact, it is so widespread and accepted that many evangelicals assume it is *the* Christian position toward Israel.[269] Yet there have been evangelical Christians who have questioned Christian Zionism since the establishment of modern Israel in 1948.

As early as 1956, O.T. Allis, a professor of Old Testament at Westminster Theological Seminary, wrote an article for *Christianity Today* titled "Israel's Transgression in Palestine."

> The attempt to restore the Jews to Palestine has proved to be unjust in itself and highly dangerous to the peace of the world. The Balfour Proclamation of 1917 was a war measure…[The British and the United Nations] have taken no adequate steps to right the wrongs of the dispossessed Arabs, whose tragic condition fosters resentment and hate throughout the Moslem world. Palestine did

## A Plea for Tough Love

not belong to the British. It did not and does not belong to the United Nations. The persecution of the Jews in Europe was a grievous act of injustice. But allowing the Jews to take possession of a large part of Palestine and to force hundreds of thousands of Arabs out of it is an equally grievous wrong.[270]

Elisabeth Elliot became well-known among Christians for her book, *Through Gates of Splendor*, the story of how her husband and four other missionaries were martyred in 1956 by the Auca Indians in Ecuador. After Israel's takeover of the West Bank in the 1967 war, she went to Jerusalem to observe the situation.

> And so the ironies piled up. The Arabs, who belonged to the land and loved it as only peasants can love it, were driven from it, and Israel pleads now for immigrants to fill their places. Israel, to prove that the land belongs to him who makes the most out of it, introduced modern agricultural methods and in certain places has made the "desert blossom." Many of the showcases of Israel—the Galilee and the Plain of Sharon, for example—were fertile to begin with. They had been cultivated for centuries by Arabs before Israel brought in tractors....
>
> I have come to the opinion that it remains for Israel alone to execute justice for those who are its responsibility. If its highways must cut through the Arabs' desert, if it claims "eminent domain," it must justly compensate those who have been displaced, those whose empty houses and lands Israel is now determined to fill with its own immigrants.[271]

In 1982 Colin Chapman published *Whose Promised Land?* This well-researched, thoughtful, and conciliatory book provided both historical information and theological interpretation. It effectively challenged preconceived ideas and simplistic understandings about Israel and Palestine. In its fifth revision, published in 2002, Chapman summarized the questions that Christians need to address:

- Are we simply dealing with "the war against terrorism"? Or are we prepared to try to understand the anger that lies behind the terrorism?...
- If the Bible seems to say that the Jews have a divine right to the land for all time, is this the only way to interpret the Bible? ...Or is there another way of reading the text which is totally faithful to scripture, but leads to a less one-sided political stance?...
- If the USA is to play the role that it is now being called upon by the rest of the world to play, what are the demands of justice?[272]

In 2002, "An Open Letter to Evangelicals and Other Interested Parties: The People of God, the Land of Israel, and the Impartiality of the Gospel" was posted on the Knox Theological College website. It was written by two faculty members of the school and signed by others. The letter boldly called for evangelical Christians to reexamine their theology:

> Lamentably, bad Christian theology is today attributing to secular Israel a divine mandate to conquer and hold Palestine, with the consequence that the Palestinian people are marginalized and regarded as virtual "Canaanites." This doctrine is both contrary to the teaching of the New Testament and a violation of the Gospel mandate. In addition, this theology puts those Christians who are urging the violent seizure and occupation of Palestinian land in moral jeopardy of their own bloodguiltiness. Are we as Christians not called to pray for and work for peace, warning both parties to this conflict that those who live by the sword will die by the sword?[273]

As important as statements from American evangelical Christians are, it is far more significant to listen to what Palestinian believers in Christ are saying about their situation. The Palestinian Kairos Document is a comprehensive statement written in 2009. The document was composed by Palestinian Christian leaders and written to the world about what is happening in Palestine:

We also declare that the Israeli occupation of Palestinian land is a sin against God and humanity because it deprives the Palestinians of their basic human rights, bestowed by God. It distorts the image of God in the Israeli who has become an occupier just as it distorts this image in the Palestinian living under occupation. We declare that any theology, seemingly based on the Bible or on faith or on history, that legitimizes the occupation, is far from Christian teachings, because it calls for violence and holy war in the name of God Almighty, subordinating God to temporary human interests, and distorting the divine image in the human beings living under both political and theological injustice....

Our message to the Jews tells them: Even though we have fought one another in the recent past and still struggle today, we are able to love and live together. We can organize our political life, with all its complexity, according to the logic of this love and its power, after ending the occupation and establishing justice.[274]

Another American plea for change comes in a letter written in September 2011 by two evangelical professors of Christian ethics, David Gushee and Glen Stassen. "An Open Letter to America's Christian Zionists" forcefully stated their concerns:

> We write as evangelical Christians committed lifelong to Israel's security, and we are seriously worried about your support for policies that violate biblical warnings about injustice and may lead to the outcome you most fear—serious harm to or even destruction of Israel.
> We write as evangelicals to you, our fellow evangelicals. On the shared basis of biblical authority, we ask you to reconsider your interpretation of Scripture, for the sake of God, humanity, the United States, and, yes, Israel itself, the Land and People we both love....
> We will leave it to God to sort out with the Jewish people of the modern state of Israel the very complex terms of his covenant with them. But we cannot remain silent about the vast array of

American Christians who support the most repressive and unjust Israeli policies in the name of Holy Land and a Holy God. We charge that you bear grave responsibility for aiding and abetting obvious sin, and if Israel once again sees war, we suggest that you will bear part of the responsibility. Christians are called to be peacemakers (Mt 5:9), but by offering uncritical support of current Israeli policies you are actively inflaming the Middle East toward war—in the name of God. This is appalling; it is intolerable; it must stop!

We plead with you, our brothers and sisters, to find a better way, a more biblical way, to love Israel. Love Israel enough to oppose rather than support actions that violate God's clearly revealed moral will. And while you are at it, it might be good to work on loving the Palestinians, some of whom are also our Christian sisters and brothers.[275]

## A Plea for Change

The time for evangelical Christians to rethink their stand toward modern Israel is long overdue. Whether one believes the Old Testament should be applied today as it was centuries ago or that the coming of Christ changes the way it should be applied, Israel's policies toward the Palestinians cannot be defended. No longer can we view Israel only through the eyeglasses of the Holocaust. Modern Israel is not a military weakling. On the contrary, it is the Goliath of the Middle East. We must examine the impact of the nation's current policies on the Palestinians. We cannot dismiss the Nakba as just a tragic but inevitable consequence of war. Israel's policies over the last sixty-five years have been deliberately oppressive.

The warning of Proverbs 24:12 is one that American evangelical Christians must take to heart when they learn what is currently taking place in Palestine and Israel.

> If you say, "But we knew nothing about this,"
>     does not he who weighs the heart perceive it?
> Does not he who guards your life know it?
>     Will he not repay everyone according to what they have done?

# A Plea for Tough Love

Out of obedience to the living God and love for both Palestinians and Israelis, we must speak out against the injustices being inflicted by the Israeli government.

Our approach should not be to turn against Israel. There is no need to choose between being pro-Israel or anti-Israel. Those are not the only two choices. Just as we can disagree with the foreign policy of the United States without being anti-American, we can also question and criticize Israel without being anti-Semitic or anti-Israel. We can be both pro-Palestinian and pro-Israeli. We can work toward security for Israel and justice for Palestine. We can be pro-peace and pro-justice.

Let's be quick to acknowledge that there are no easy answers to the Palestinian-Israeli conflict. To pretend otherwise would be naïve. The future will be difficult, and forging peace will require extraordinary effort and courageous perseverance. But we must start by giving up our unquestioning, uncritical, unconditional, and *sinful* support for Israel's policies.

It is time that our love becomes tough. For the good of Israel, Palestine, and America, and for the honor of the God of justice and love, that is my plea.

Connect with the author at:
apleafortoughlove@gmail.com

# Glossary

### BALFOUR DECLARATION
The British Foreign Secretary Arthur Balfour wrote a letter on November 2, 1917, that included a statement about Britain's favorable disposition toward "the establishment in Palestine of a national home for the Jewish people." It also stated that "nothing shall be done which may prejudice the civil and religious rights of existing non-Jewish communities in Palestine." This letter is known as the Balfour Declaration.

### CAMP DAVID
Meetings at the US presidential retreat site known as Camp David can refer to two different series of negotiations that took place there. In 1979 President Carter successfully worked with Israeli Prime Minister Menachem Begin and Egyptian President Anwar Sadat to sign the first Arab-Israeli peace agreement. Negotiations in 2000 at Camp David between President Clinton, Israeli Prime Minister Ehud Barak, and Palestinian Authority President Yassar Arafat failed to produce any agreement and led to intensified conflict between Israelis and Palestinians.

### CHRISTIAN ZIONISM
Christian Zionists are evangelical Christians who support the establishment of a national state for the Jewish people in their ancient homeland. Moreover, they understand the Bible to teach that all believers in Christ should be strongly pro-Israel.

### COVENANT THEOLOGY
According to Covenant or Reformed Theology, the Old Testament has been fulfilled in Jesus Christ and his church. Through Jesus, the sharp distinction between Israel and the church has been overcome; the people of God now include both believing Jews and Gentiles. Covenant theologians may be but are not necessarily Christian Zionists.

## Dispensationalism

In contrast to Covenant Theology, this school of theology insists on a sharp distinction between Israel and the church. Unfulfilled Old Testament prophecies will be literally fulfilled after Christ raptures his church to heaven and resumes his work with the physical descendants of Abraham. Almost all dispensationalists are staunch Christian Zionists.

## Fourth Geneva Convention

The Geneva Conventions of 1949 were passed by the United Nations to create standards for the humanitarian treatment of prisoners, civilians, and the wounded during wartime. The Fourth Geneva Convention forbids an occupying power from transferring members of its civilian population into the territory it occupies.

## Fulfillment Theology

Proponents of this theological approach maintain that the New Testament teaches that the promises of the Old Testament have been fulfilled in Jesus Christ. Jewish and Gentile believers have now become the people of God. God does still have a plan for the future salvation of the Jewish people, and anti-Semitism should have no place in Christian practice.

## Haganah

Prior to Israel's establishment in 1948, the Haganah was the major Zionist paramilitary organization.

## Intifada

In Arabic, the word *intifada* means "shaking off." It refers to popular Palestinian movements of protest against the Israeli occupation of Palestine. The First Intifada began in 1987 and continued into 1991. The Second Intifada, also known as the al-Aqsa Intifada, is dated from 2000 to 2005.

## Irgun

Prior to 1948 the Irgun was a Zionist paramilitary group. In contrast to the Haganah, the Irgun advocated an aggressive policy toward the British and Arabs.

# GLOSSARY

### KAIROS PALESTINE DOCUMENT
In 2009 Christian leaders in Palestine issued this formal declaration asking the world to address the displacement and suffering caused by the Israeli occupation of Palestine.

### KNESSET
The national legislature in the Israeli parliamentarian system of government is called the Knesset. It may be thought of as the Israeli equivalent of the United States Congress.

### NAKBA
This Arabic term means "catastrophe" and is used by Palestinians to describe the 1948 war that led to the displacement of Arabs from their homes and produced 700,000 Arab refugees.

### OSLO ACCORDS
With a famous handshake on the White House lawn in 1993, Israeli Prime Minister Yitzhak Rabin and Palestine Liberation Organization Chairman Yasser Arafat agreed to a set of principles that had been secretly negotiated in Oslo, Norway. The Oslo Accords set out a five-year process for the establishment of a Palestinian state. Greeted initially with great fanfare and hope, the Oslo Accords eventually complicated the situation and produced increased strife.

### REPLACEMENT THEOLOGY
Christian Zionists describe Replacement Theology as a theological system which claims that the church has replaced Israel in the plan of God. Critics of Replacement Theology maintain that it is mistaken because it does not interpret the Old Testament literally and because it usually leads to anti-Semitism.

### STERN GANG
Prior to 1948 the Stern Gang, also known as Lehi, was a Zionist paramilitary group. In contrast to the Haganah, the Stern Gang advocated an aggressive policy toward the British and Arabs.

## United Nations General Assembly Resolution 181

Passed on November 29, 1947, this UN General Assembly resolution called for the partition of the land into two states—Israel and Palestine. The Israelis accepted the plan; the Arabs rejected it.

## United Nations General Assembly Resolution 194

Passed on December 11, 1948, this resolution addressed the problem of Palestinian refugees following the 1948 War: "…the refugees wishing to return to their homes and live at peace with their neighbours should be permitted to do so." It also called on Israel to provide financial compensation to those not choosing to return. Israel refused to abide by this resolution.

## United Nations Security Council Resolution 242

On November 22, 1967, the UN Security Council passed this resolution, which called for the "termination of all claims or states of belligerency and respect for and acknowledgement of the sovereignty, territorial integrity and political independence of every State in the area and their right to live in peace within secure and recognized boundaries free from threats or acts of violence." Yasser Arafat, the leader of the Palestine Liberation Organization, accepted the resolution on September 13, 1993, recognizing Israel's right to exist and renouncing terrorism.

The resolution also called for the "withdrawal of Israeli armed forces from territories occupied in the recent conflict." Israel disputes the meaning of "territories," arguing that the resolution does not forbid the establishment of settlements in the West Bank even though the Israeli Foreign Ministry legal counsel, Theodor Meron, indicated in 1967 that "civilian settlement in the administered territories contravenes explicit provisions of the Fourth Geneva Convention."

## Zionism

This movement takes its name from Mount Zion in Jerusalem, the hill upon which the temple of God once stood. Theodor Herzl (1860–1904) is considered the father of Zionism because he began the movement to create a national homeland for Jews.

# Endnotes

[1] Hal Lindsey, *The Late Great Planet Earth* (Grand Rapids, MI: Zondervan Publishing House, 1970), 184.

[2] On the influence of these two books see Melani McAlister, *Epic Encounters* (Berkeley, CA: University of California Press, 2001), 159–178.

[3] For a one-volume presentation of both the Israeli and Palestinian narratives, see Dan Cohn-Sherbok and Dawoud El-Alami, *The Palestine-Israeli Conflict: A Beginner's Guide*, 3rd ed. (Oxford: Oneworld Publications, 2008).

[4] "Demographics of Israel: Jewish & Non-Jewish Population of Israel/Palestine," Jewish Virtual Library, accessed July 21, 2015, https://www.jewishvirtuallibrary.org/jsource/Society_&_Culture/israel_palestine_pop.html.

[5] StandWithUs, *Israel 101* (Los Angeles, CA: StandWithUs, 2010), 11, accessed July 26, 2013, http://www.standwithus.com/booklets/IL101International/.

[6] Quoted in Benny Morris, *Righteous Victims* (New York: Vintage Books, 2001), 23.

[7] Colin Chapman, *Whose Promised Land?* (Grand Rapids, MI: Baker Book House, 2002), 54.

[8] Benny Morris, *Righteous Victims* (New York: Vintage Books, 2001), 24.

[9] Iain H. Murray, *The Puritan Hope* (Carlisle, PA: Banner of Truth Trust, 1971), 41.

[10] Henry Drummond, *Dialogues on Prophecy* (London: James Nisbet, 1828), ii-iii, quoted in Stephen Sizer, *Christian Zionism* (Downers Grove, IL: InterVarsity Press, 2004), 45.

[11] Quoted in Benny Morris, *Righteous Victims* (New York: Vintage Books, 2001), 75.

[12] Timothy P. Weber, *On the Road to Armageddon* (Grand Rapids, MI: Baker Book House, 2004), 159.

[13] Morris, *Righteous Victims*, 107, 122.

[14] Ibid., 129.

[15] Cohn-Sherbok and Dawoud El-Alami, *The Palestine-Israeli Conflict: A Beginner's Guide*, 3rd ed. (Oxford: Oneworld Publications, 2008), 39.

[16] Benny Morris, *Righteous Victims* (New York: Vintage Books, 2001), 158.
[17] Ibid., 182–183.
[18] Cohn-Sherbok and Dawoud El-Alami, *The Palestine-Israeli Conflict: A Beginner's Guide*, 3rd ed. (Oxford: Oneworld Publications, 2008), 52–53.
[19] Marvin J. Rosenthal, "A Nation Reborn through the Faithful Hand of God," *Zion's Fire*, March-April 2013, 18.
[20] Marvin J. Rosenthal, "The Peace before the Storm," *Zion's Fire*, March-April 2013, 25. See also StandWithUs, *Israel 101*, 9.
[21] David Dolan, *Holy War for the Promised Land* (Nashville, TN: Broadman & Holman Publishers, 2003), 98-100.
[22] Marvin J. Rosenthal, "A Nation Reborn through the Faithful Hand of God," *Zion's Fire*, March-April 2013, 21.
[23] State of Palestine, "The Palestine National Charter of 1964," accessed June 24, 2013, http://www.un.int/wcm /content/site /palestine/pid/12363.
[24] Cohn-Sherbok and Dawoud El-Alami, *The Palestine-Israeli Conflict: A Beginner's Guide*, 3rd ed. (Oxford: Oneworld Publications, 2008), 69.
[25] Ibid., 71-72.
[26] Ibid., 73-74; Benny Morris, *Righteous Victims* (New York: Vintage Books, 2001), 346.
[27] Cohn-Sherbok and Dawoud El-Alami, *The Palestine-Israeli Conflict: A Beginner's Guide*, 3rd ed. (Oxford: Oneworld Publications, 2008), 77-78; Benny Morris, *Righteous Victims* (New York: Vintage Books, 2001), 449.
[28] Cohn-Sherbok and Dawoud El-Alami, *The Palestine-Israeli Conflict: A Beginner's Guide*, 3rd ed. (Oxford: Oneworld Publications, 2008), 84; Benny Morris, *Righteous Victims* (New York: Vintage Books, 2001), 577-578.
[29] United Nations Security Council, "Resolution 242 (1967) of 22 November 1967," accessed September 13, 2013, http://unispal.un.org/unispal.nsf/0/7D35E1F729DF491C85256EE700686136.
[30] Cohn-Sherbok and Dawoud El-Alami, *The Palestine-Israeli Conflict: A Beginner's Guide*, 3rd ed. (Oxford: Oneworld Publications, 2008), 92-93; Benny Morris, *Righteous Victims* (New York: Vintage Books, 2001), 623.
[31] Cohn-Sherbok and Dawoud El-Alami, *The Palestine-Israeli Conflict: A Beginner's Guide*, 3rd ed. (Oxford: Oneworld Publications, 2008), 104-105; Benny Morris, *Righteous Victims* (New York: Vintage Books, 2001), 659.

# ENDNOTES

[32] Cohn-Sherbok and Dawoud El-Alami, *The Palestine-Israeli Conflict: A Beginner's Guide*, 3rd ed. (Oxford: Oneworld Publications, 2008), 113.

[33] Ibid., 122.

[34] Efraim Karsh, "What Occupation?" *Commentary*, July – August 2002, accessed July 26, 2013, http://www.aish.com/jw/me/48898917.html.

[35] David Dolan, *Holy War for the Promised Land* (Nashville, TN: Broadman & Holman Publishers, 2003), 229.

[36] Sean Young, "Ahmadinejad: Destroy Israel, End Crisis," *The Washington Post*, August 3, 2006.

[37] Council on Foreign Relations, "Netanyahu's Address to U.S. Congress, May 2011." May 24, 2011, accessed June 25, 2013, http://www.cfr.org/israel/netanyahus-address-us-congress-may-2011/p25073.

[38] For a comprehensive treatment of the Palestinian viewpoint, see Alex Awad, *Palestinian Memories* (Bethlehem: Bethlehem Bible College, 2012). Awad is the pastor of the international East Jerusalem Baptist Church in Jerusalem and Dean of Students at Bethlehem Bible College. See also Cohn-Sherbok and Dawoud El-Alami, *The Palestine-Israeli Conflict: A Beginner's Guide*, 3rd ed. (Oxford: Oneworld Publications, 2008).

[39] Benny Morris, *Righteous Victims* (New York: Vintage Books, 2001), 42. Shaftesbury's actual words were apparently: "A country without a nation for a nation without a country." See Stephen Sizer, *Christian Zionism* (Downers Grove, IL: InterVarsity Press, 2004), 55-60; Victoria Clark, *Allies for Armageddon* (New Haven, CT: Yale University Press), 66-72.

[40] Ahad Ha'am quoted in Rabbi Michael Lerner, *Embracing Israel / Palestine* (Berkeley, CA: North Atlantic Books, 2012), 65.

[41] Benny Morris, *Righteous Victims* (New York: Vintage Books, 2001), 57.

[42] Avi Shlaim, *The Iron Wall* rev. ed. (New York: W.W. Norton & Company, 2014), 3.

[43] Shlomo Ben-Ami, *Scars of War, Wounds of Peace* (New York: Oxford University Press, 2006), 25.

[44] Theodore Herzl quoted in Ilan Pappe, *The Ethnic Cleansing of Palestine* (Oxford: OneWorld Publications, 2006), 250, 281 n.2.

[45] Israel Zangwell quoted ibid.

[46] Menachem Usshiskin quoted in Brant Rosen, *Wrestling in the Daylight*

(Charlottesville, VA: Just World Books, 2012), 186.

[47] David Ben-Gurion quoted in Pappe, *The Ethnic Cleansing*, xi.

[48] David Ben-Gurion quoted in John J. Mearsheimer and Stephen M. Walt, *The Israel Lobby and U.S. Foreign Policy* (New York: Farrar, Straus and Giroux, 2007), 95.

[49] Morris, *Righteous Victims*, 254.

[50] Lord Balfour quoted in Stephen Sizer, *Christian Zionism* (Downers Grove, IL: InterVarsity Press, 2004), 64–65.

[51] Quoted in Colin Chapman, *Whose Promised Land?* (Grand Rapids, MI: Baker Book House, 2002), 66.

[52] "Alexandria Protocol," quoted in Benny Morris, *Righteous Victims* (New York: Vintage Books, 2001), 172. This statement issued by Arab leaders in 1945, said, "…for there can be no greater injustice and aggression than solving the problem of the Jews of Europe by…inflicting injustice on the Palestine Arabs."

[53] Arthur Koestler, *Promise and Fulfilment* (London: Macmillan, 1949), 4, quoted in Colin Chapman, *Whose Promised Land?* (Grand Rapids, MI: Baker Book House, 2002), 66.

[54] Benny Morris, *1948 and After: Israel and the Palestinians* (New York: Oxford University Press, 2003), 13, quoted in John J. Mearsheimer and Stephen M. Walt, *The Israel Lobby and U.S. Foreign Policy* (New York: Farrar, Straus and Giroux, 2007), 81. See also Rashid Khalidi, *The Iron Cage* (Boston, MA: Beacon Press, 2007), xxxix.

[55] Morris, *Righteous Victims*, 216-217.

[56] Benny Morris, *1948 and After: Israel and the Palestinians* (New York: Oxford University Press, 2003), 15, quoted in John J. Mearsheimer and Stephen M. Walt, *The Israel Lobby and U.S. Foreign Policy* (New York: Farrar, Straus and Giroux, 2007), 82.

[57] Shlomo Ben-Ami, *Scars of War, Wounds of Peace* (New York: Oxford University Press, 2006), 39.

[58] Ibid., 55.

[59] The unaccounted 5.9% of the land was classified as "state land" under the British Mandate.

[60] *A Survey of Palestine* (Jerusalem: British Government Printer, 1945-1946), quoted in Awad, *Palestinian Memories*, 110.

## Endnotes

[61] Ari Shavit, *My Promised Land* (New York: Spiegel & Grau, 2013), 49.

[62] "Plan Dalet," March 10, 1948, quoted in Ilan Pappe, *Ethnic Cleansing* (Oxford: Oneworld Publications, 2007), 39.

[63] The estimated number of villages destroyed ranges from 350 to over 500. The difficulty in arriving at a precise number comes from the criteria used for determining what a village is. Meron Benvenisti, *Sacred Landscapes* (Berkeley, CA: University of California Press, 2000), 80; Ben White, *Israeli Apartheid* (New York: Pluto Press, 2009), 33, 55.

[64] Benny Morris, *Righteous Victims* (New York: Vintage Books, 2001), 209.

[65] Ilan Pappe, *Ethnic Cleansing* (Oxford: Oneworld Publications, 2007), 119.

[66] David Ben-Gurion *Rebirth and Destiny of Israel* (New York: Philosophical Library, 1954), 530-531, quoted in Colin Chapman, *Whose Promised Land?* (Grand Rapids, MI: Baker Book House, 2002), 74.

[67] Meron Benvenisti, *Sacred Landscapes* (Berkeley, CA: University of California Press, 2000), 150.

[68] Shlomo Ben-Ami, *Scars of War, Wounds of Peace* (New York: Oxford University Press, 2006), 46.

[69] Count Folke Bernadotte quoted in Alex Awad, *Palestinian Memories* (Bethlehem: Bethlehem Bible College, 2012), 113.

[70] Saree Makdisi, *Palestine Inside Out* (New York: W.W. Norton & Company, 2008), 255-256; Ilan Pappe, *Ethnic Cleansing* (Oxford: Oneworld Publications, 2007), 156-157; Cohn-Sherbok and Dawoud El-Alami, *The Palestine-Israeli Conflict: A Beginner's Guide*, 3rd ed. (Oxford: Oneworld Publications, 2008), 183.

[71] UN General Assembly, "194 (III). Palestine — Progress Report of the United Nations Mediator." December 11, 1948, accessed July 26, 2013, http://unispal.un.org/UNISPAL.NSF/0/C758572B78D1CD0085256BCF0077E51A.

[72] Rabbi Michael Lerner, *Embracing Israel / Palestine* (Berkeley, CA: North Atlantic Books, 2012), 395-396.

[73] Christopher Hitchens, "Broadcasts," in Edward W. Said and Christopher Hitchens, *Blaming the Victims* (London: Verso, 1988), 73-83.

[74] For a variety of opinions, see Colin Chapman, *Whose Promised Land?* (Grand Rapids, MI: Baker Book House, 2002), 77-80.

[75] Benny Morris, "Revising the Palestinian Exodus of 1948," quoted in Eugene L. Rogan and Avi Shlaim, eds. *The War for Palestine: Rewriting the History of 1948* (Cambridge: Cambridge University Press, 2001), 38, quoted in Marda Dunsky, *Pens and Swords* (New York: Columbia University Press, 2008), 72.

[76] Moshe Dayan quoted in *Haaretz*, April 4, 1969, quoted in Colin Chapman, *Whose Promised Land?* (Grand Rapids, MI: Baker Book House, 2002), 196-197.

[77] Shlomo Ben-Ami, *Scars of War, Wounds of Peace* (New York: Oxford University Press, 2006), 42.

[78] Yitzhak Rabin quoted in A. and L. Cockburn, *Dangerous Liaisons: The Inside Story of the Covert U.S.-Israeli Relationship* (Oxford: Lion Publishing), 153-154, quoted in Alex Awad, *Palestinian Memories* (Bethlehem: Bethlehem Bible College, 2012), 127. Some Israeli generals opposed Israel's attack. See also Miko Peled, *The General's Son* (Charlottesville, VA: Just World Books, 2012), 43-44.

[79] Israel Ministry of Foreign Affairs, "Address by Prime Minister Begin at the National Defense College." August 8 1982, accessed May 13, 2013, http://www.mfa.gov.il/mfa/foreignpolicy/mfadocuments/yearbook6/pages/55%20address%20by%20prime%20minister%20begin%20at%20the%20national.aspx.

[80] Gershom Gorenberg, "Israel's Tragedy Foretold," *New York Times*, March 10, 2006, accessed February 5, 2013, http://www.nytimes.com/2006/03/10/opinion/10gorenberg.html?pagewanted=all&_r=0.

[81] Benny Morris, *Righteous Victims* (New York: Vintage Books, 2001), 565.

[82] Ibid., 341.

[83] Rabbi Michael Lerner, *Embracing Israel / Palestine* (Berkeley, CA: North Atlantic Books, 2012), 178-179.

[84] King Abdullah II, *Our Last Best Chance* (New York: Viking, 2011), 189.

[85] Rabbi Michael Lerner, *Embracing Israel / Palestine* (Berkeley, CA: North Atlantic Books, 2012), 198-199.

[86] "The Arab Peace Initiative, 2002," accessed August 4, 2015, http://www.al-bab.com /arab/docs/league/peace02.htm.

[87] King Abdullah II, *Our Last Best Chance* (New York: Viking, 2011), 206.

[88] Alex Awad, *Palestinian Memories* (Bethlehem: Bethlehem Bible College, 2012), 237.

[89] Avi Shlaim, *The Iron Wall*, rev. ed. (New York: W.W. Norton & Company, 2014), 740.

[90] Naomi Chazan, "Stop Saying No to the Best Deal Ever," *The Times of Israel*, May 5, 2013, accessed July 26, 2013, http://blogs.timesofisrael.com/stop-saying-no-to-the-best-deal-ever.

[91] Cohn-Sherbok and Dawoud El-Alami, *The Palestine-Israeli Conflict: A Beginner's Guide*, 3rd ed. (Oxford: Oneworld Publications, 2008), 257-258.

[92] For an examination of the impact of Christian tourism in the Holy Land, see Stephen Sizer, *Christian Zionism* (Downers Grove, IL: InterVarsity Press, 2004), 216-219.

[93] Shlomo Ben-Ami, *Scars of War, Wounds of Peace* (New York: Oxford University Press, 2006), 332.

[94] Council on Foreign Relations, "Netanyahu's Address to U.S. Congress, May 2011."

[95] Dan Rabinowitz and Khawla Abut-Baker, *Coffins on Our Shoulders* (Berkeley, CA: University of California Press, 2005), 54; Ben White, *Israeli Apartheid* (New York: Pluto Press, 2009), 42-44; Saree Makdisi, *Palestine Inside Out* (New York: W.W. Norton & Company, 2008), 144-146.

[96] Ben White, *Israeli Apartheid* (New York: Pluto Press, 2009), 49; Saree Makdisi, *Palestine Inside Out* (New York: W.W. Norton & Company, 2008), 147; Adalah, "The Inequality Report: The Palestinian Arab Minority in Israel," 9. March 2011, accessed January 23, 2015, http://www.adalah.org/uploads/oldfiles/upfiles/2011/Adalah_ The_Inequality_Report_March_2011.pdf.

[97] Meron Benvenisti, *Sacred Landscapes* (Berkeley, CA: University of California Press, 2000), 159.

[98] B'Tselem, "By Hook and by Crook: Israeli Settlement Policy in the West Bank." July 2010, 21-35, accessed January 23, 2015, http://www.btselem.org/download/201007_by_hook_and_by_crook_ eng.pdf.

[99] Ben White, *Israeli Apartheid* (New York: Pluto Press, 2009), 56; Ben White, *Palestinians in Israel* (London: Pluto Press, 2012), 30-32.

[100] Ben White, *Israeli Apartheid* (New York: Pluto Press, 2009), 55, 80-82; Ben White, *Palestinians in Israel* (London: Pluto Press, 2012), 42-44; Saree

Makdisi, *Palestine Inside Out* (New York: W.W. Norton & Company, 2008), 148; Ilan Pappe, *The Forgotten Palestinians* (New Haven, CT: Yale University Press, 2011), 209, 210-212.

[101] Ben White, *Israeli Apartheid* (New York: Pluto Press, 2009), 50; Ben White, *Palestinians in Israel* (London: Pluto Press, 2012), 48-50, 92; Gershom Gorenberg, *The Unmaking of Israel* (New York: HarperCollins Publishers, 2011), 208-209.

[102] Ben White, *Israeli Apartheid* (New York: Pluto Press, 2009), 55; Adalah, *The Inequality Report*, 16.

[103] Saree Makdisi, *Palestine Inside Out* (New York: W.W. Norton & Company, 2008), 150-151.

[104] Ben White, *Israeli Apartheid* (New York: Pluto Press, 2009), 53.

[105] The Orr Commission, "The Official Summation of the Orr Commission Report," trans. by *Haaretz*, September 2, 2003, accessed July 28, 2013, http://www.uktaskforce.org/docs/the-official-summation-of-the-orr-commission-report.pdf.

[106] Geoffrey Aronson, "Recapitulating the Redeployments: The Israel-PLO 'Interim Agreements,'" April 27, 2000, accessed July 28, 2013, http://www.thejerusalemfund.org/ht/display/ContentDetails/i/2151/pid/v.

[107] B'Tselem, "Acting the Landlord: Israel's Policy in Area C, the West Bank." June 2013, 7, accessed January 23, 2015, http://www.btselem.org/download/201306_area_c_report_eng.pdf.

[108] United Nations Office for the Coordination of Humanitarian Affairs, "Movement and Access in the West Bank." September 2011, accessed January 23, 2015, http://www.ochaopt.org/documents/ocha_opt_movementandaccess_factsheet_september_2011.pdf.

[109] United Nations Office for the Coordination of Humanitarian Affairs, "The Humanitarian Impact of the Barrier." July 2012, accessed January 23, 2015, http://www.ochaopt.org/documents/ocha_opt_barrier_factsheet_july_2012_english.pdf; René Backmann, *A Wall in Palestine*, trans. A. Kaiser (New York: Picador, 2010), 66.

[110] B'Tselem, "Palestinians with work permits must arrive at checkpoints before dawn, undergo humiliating inspection," July 1, 2013, accessed January 23, 2015, http://www.btselem.org/workers/20130701_conditions_in_eyal_and_tarqumya_checkpoints.

# Endnotes

[111] United Nations Office for the Coordination of Humanitarian Affairs, "The Humanitarian Impact of the Barrier." July 2012.

[112] Amos Harel, "Shin Bet: Palestinian Truce Main Cause for Reduced Terror," *Haaretz*, January 2, 2006, accessed January 12, 2014, http://www.haaretz.com/print-edition/news/shin-bet-palestinian-truce-main-cause-for-reduced-terror-1.61607; Ben White, "Did Israeli Apartheid Wall Really Stop Suicide Bombings?" January 10, 2014, accessed January 10, 2014, http://electronicintifada.net/blogs/ben-white/did-israeli-apartheid-wall-really-stop-suicide-bombings.

[113] United Nations Office for the Coordination of Humanitarian Affairs, "The Humanitarian Impact of the Barrier." July 2012.

[114] Congressional Research Service. *Israel: Background and U.S. Relations*, by Jim Zanotti. December 8, 2014, 47.

[115] B'Tselem, "By Hook and by Crook:Israeli Settlement Policy in the West Bank." July 2010, 21–35, accessed January 23, 2015, http://www.btselem,org.download/201007_by_hook_by_crook_eng.pdf..

[116] *CIA Factbook,* quoted in Congressional Research Service, *Israel: Background and U.S. Relations*, by Jim Zanotti, 46, n. 146. December 8, 2014, accessed January 23, 2015, http://www.fas.org/sgp/crs/mideast/RL33476.pdf.

[117] United Nations Office for the Coordination of Humanitarian Affairs. "East Jerusalem: Key Humanitarian Concerns." December 2012, accessed January 23, 2015, http://www.ochaopt.org/documents/ocha_opt_jerusalem_factsheet_december_2012_english.pdf.

[118] United Nations Office for the Coordination of Humanitarian Affairs, "The Humanitarian Impact of Israeli Settlement Policies." December 2012, accessed January 23, 2015, http://www.ochaopt.org/documents/ocha_opt_settlements_factsheet_december_2012_english.pdf.

[119] "Daher's Vineyard Land History," *Tent of the Nations*, accessed September 21, 2013, http://www.tentofnations .org /about/dahers-vineyard-land-history; Mitri Raheb, *I Am a Palestinian Christian* (Minneapolis, MN: Fortress Press, 1995), 47-52; Alex Awad, *Palestinian Memories* (Bethlehem: Bethlehem Bible College, 2012), 210-212; Ilene Prusher, "The Tree Uprooting Heard around the World," *Haaretz,* June 12, 2014, accessed June 15, 2014, http://www.haaretz.com/news/features/.premium-1.598272.

[120] Alex Awad, *Palestinian Memories* (Bethlehem: Bethlehem Bible College, 2012), 135; Ben White, *Israeli Apartheid* (New York: Pluto Press, 2009), 73, 77-78.

[121] United Nations Office for the Coordination of Humanitarian Affairs, "The Humanitarian Impact of Israeli Settlement Policies." December 2012.

[122] B'Tselem, "Israel Holding More Than 470 Palestinians in Administrative Detention—Highest Number in 5 Years," October 7, 2014, accessed January 23, 2015, http://www.btselem.org/administrative_detention/20141007_spike_in_number_of_administrative_detainees.

[123] United Nations Office for the Coordination of Humanitarian Affairs, "Demolitions and Forced Displacement in the Occupied West Bank." January 2012, accessed January 23, 2015, http://www.ochaopt.org/documents/ocha_opt_demolitions_factsheet_january_2012_english.pdf.

[124] Amnesty International, "Israel and the Occupied Territories: Under the Rubble: House Demolition and Destruction of Land and Property," May 2004, 14, accessed July 28, 2013, http://www.ochaopt.org/documents/opt_prot_amnestyint_under_the_rubble_may_2004.pdf.

[125] Saree Makdisi, *Palestine Inside Out* (New York: W.W. Norton & Company, 2008), 5-6.

[126] Congressional Research Service, *Israel: Background and U.S. Relations*, by Jim Zanotti, 17, June 1, 2015, accessed August 13, 2015.

[127] Ben White, *Israeli Apartheid* (New York: Pluto Press, 2009), 113.

[128] United Nations Office for the Coordination of Humanitarian Affairs, "Five Years of Blockade: The Humanitarian Situation in the Gaza Strip." June 2012, accessed January 23, 2015, http://www.ochaopt.org/documents/ocha_opt_gaza_blockade_factsheet_june_2012_english.pdf.

[129] United Nations Office for the Coordination of Humanitarian Affairs, "Access Restricted Areas (ARA) in the Gaza Strip." July 2013, accessed January 23, 2015, http://www.ochaopt.org/documents /ocha_opt_gaza_ara_factsheet_july_2013_english.pdf; "The Gaza Strip: The Humanitarian Impact of Movement Restrictions on People and Goods." July 2013, accessed January 23, 2015, http://www.ochaopt.org/documents/ocha_opt_gaza_blockade_ factsheet_july_2013_english.pdf.

## Endnotes

[130] United Nations Office for the Coordination of Humanitarian Affairs, "The Humanitarian Impact of Gaza's Electricity and Fuel Crisis." March 2014, accessed January 23, 2015, http://www.ochaopt.org/documents/ocha_opt_electricity_factsheet_march_2014_english.pdf.

[131] "Secretary-General's Remarks at the Cairo Conference on Palestine," United Nations. October 12, 2014, accessed January 23, 2015, http://www.un.org/sg/statements/index.asp?nid=8099.

[132] Miko Peled, *The General's Son* (Charlottesville, VA: Just World Books, 2012), 159.

[133] Rabbi Michael Lerner, *Embracing Israel / Palestine* (Berkeley, CA: North Atlantic Books, 2012), 214.

[134] For a more complete treatment of these subjects, see Alex Awad, *Palestinian Memories* (Bethlehem: Bethlehem Bible College, 2012), 292-306, 313-315.

[135] Benny Morris, *Righteous Victims* (New York: Vintage Books, 2001), 147.

[136] Yossi Said, "Are Begin and Shamir Also Considered Terrorists?" *Haaretz*, June 24, 2011, accessed July 28, 2013, http://www.haaretz.com/print-edition/opinion/are-begin-and-shamir-also-considered-terrorists-1.369342.

[137] Alex Awad, *Palestinian Memories* (Bethlehem: Bethlehem Bible College, 2012), 292-299.

[138] "Rice Calls on Israel to Take Bold Steps for Peace," *The Chosen Ilbo*. 5 November 2007, accessed July 20, 2013, http://english.chosun.com/site/data/html_dir/2007/11/05/2007110561032.html.

[139] Alex Awad, *Palestinian Memories* (Bethlehem: Bethlehem Bible College, 2012), 313-315.

[140] Colin Chapman, "A Christian Response to Radical Islam," (lecture, Christ at the Checkpoint, March 2012), accessed September 21, 2013, http://danutm.files.wordpress.com/2012/03/colin-chapman-a-christian-response-to-radical-islam.pdf.

[141] Munther Isaac, "Palestinian Christians React to Israeli Ambassador's Claims about Holy Land Churches," *Sojourners*, 27 March 2012, accessed September 18, 2013, http://sojo.net/blogs/2012/03/27/palestinian-christians-react-israeli-ambassador%E2%80%99s-claims-about-holy-land-churches.

[142] Alex Awad, *Palestinian Memories* (Bethlehem:Bethlehem Bible College, 2012), 304.

[143] Shlomo Ben-Ami, *Scars of War, Wounds of Peace* (New York: Oxford University Press, 2006), 212.

[144] Avraham Burg, *The Holocaust is Over: We Must Rise from Its Ashes* (New York: Palgrave Macmillan, 2008), 83-84.

[145] Henry Siegman, "The Great Middle East Peace Process Scam," *London Review of Books*, August 2007, 16.

[146] Mark Braverman, "Ana Falastini Yehudi: I Am a Palestinian Jew," *Cornerstone*, Issue 56—Spring 2010, 16.

[147] Colin Chapman, *Whose Promised Land?* (Grand Rapids, MI: Baker Book House, 2002), 254-256; Stephen Sizer, *Christian Zionism* (Downers Grove, IL: InterVarsity Press, 2004), 19-24; Alex Awad, *Palestinian Memories* (Bethlehem: Bethlehem Bible College, 2012), 244.

[148] Koenig lists 57 catastrophes and events that he claims took place as a result of Presidents George H.W. Bush, Bill Clinton, and George W. Bush pressuring Israel to trade land for peace. William Koenig, *Eye to Eye—Facing the Consequences of Dividing Israel* (Alexandria, VA: About Him Publishing, 2007).

[149] John Hagee, *In Defense of Israel* (Lake Mary, FL: FrontLine, 2007), 111.

[150] Victoria Clark, *Allies for Armageddon* (New Haven, CT: Yale University Press), 12.

[151] D.A. Carson, *For the Love of God* (Wheaton, IL: Crossway Books, 1998), 1: May 4.

[152] R.T. France, *Jesus and the Old Testament* (Grand Rapids, MI: Baker Book House, 1971), 75-76.

[153] See David E. Holwerda, *Jesus & Israel* (Grand Rapids, MI: Eerdmans, 1995), 85-112; O. Palmer Robertson, *The Israel of God* (Phillipsburg, NJ: P&R Publishing, 2000), 3-31; Gary Burge, *Jesus and the Land* (Grand Rapids, MI: Baker Publishing Group, 2010).

[154] John Hagee, *In Defense of Israel* (Lake Mary, FL: FrontLine, 2007), 167.

[155] A.A. MacRae, "*('ōl m), forever, ever, everlasting, evermore, perpetual, old, ancient, world*" in *Theological Word Book of the Old Testament*, ed. R. Laird Harris, Gleason J. Archer, Jr. and Bruce K. Waltke (Chicago: Moody Press, 1980), #1631.

[156] Bruce Waltke, *An Old Testament Theology* (Grand Rapids, MI: Zondervan, 2007), 439.

[157] William E. Blackstone, *Jesus is Coming* (London, Fleming H. Revell,

## Endnotes

1908), 235 quoted in Victoria Clark, *Allies for Armageddon* (New Haven, CT: Yale University Press), 93.

[158] Walter C. Kaiser, Jr., *Preaching and Teaching the Last Things* (Grand Rapids, MI: Baker, 2011), 82.

[159] Tim LaHaye and Jerry Jenkins, *Are We Living in the Last Days?* (Wheaton, IL: Tyndale House Publishers, 1999), 5.

[160] See Timothy Paul Jones, *Rose Guide to End-Times Prophecy* (Torrance, CA: Rose Publishing, Inc., 2011), 263-269.

[161] Tim LaHaye and Jerry Jenkins, *Are We Living in the Last Days?* (Wheaton, IL: Tyndale House Publishers, 1999), 84.

[162] Peter Craigie, *Ezekiel* (Philadelphia: The Westminster Press, 1983), 265.

[163] Ralph Alexander, "Ezekiel," in *The Expositor's Bible Commentary*, ed. Frank E. Gaebelein (Grand Rapids, MI: Zondervan, 1986), 6:938.

[164] Daniel I. Block, *The Book of Ezekiel, Chapters 25-48* (Grand Rapids, MI: Eerdmans, 1998), 494.

[165] J.A. Montgomery, *A Critical and Exegetical Commentary on the Book of Daniel* (Edinburgh: T. & T. Clark, 1927), 400.

[166] Jerome, *Commentary on Daniel*, trans. G.L. Archer (Grand Rapids, MI: Baker Book House, 1958), 95; quoted in Gleason L. Archer, Jr., "Daniel" in *The Expositor's Bible Commentary*, ed. Frank E. Gaebelein (Grand Rapids, MI: Zondervan Publishing House, 1985), 120.

[167] Robert D. Culver, *Daniel and the Latter Days* (Westwood, NJ: Fleming H. Revell Company, 1954), 135.

[168] Dwight Wilson, *Armageddon Now!* (Tyler, TX: Institute for Christian Economics, 1991), 124-126; Stephen Sizer, *Christian Zionism* (Downers Grove, IL: InterVarsity Press, 2004), 151-153; Timothy P. Weber, *On the Road to Armageddon* (Grand Rapids, MI: Baker Book House, 2004), 168-169; Caitlin Carenen, *The Fervent Embrace* (New York: New York University Press, 2012), 30, 120.

[169] Marvin J. Rosenthal, "Can These Bones Live?" *Zion's Fire*, March-April 2013, 13.

[170] International Christian Embassy in Jerusalem, "'An Open Letter to America's Christian Zionists,' A Response by the International Christian Embassy Jerusalem." October 5, 2011, accessed July 14, 2013, http://us.icej.org/sites/default/files/en/pdf/icej_cz_open_letter_response_oct2011_0.pdf.

171 For a brief survey of key prophetic texts, see C. Marvin Pate and Calvin B. Haines, Jr., *Doomsday Delusions* (Downers Grove, IL: InterVarsity Press, 1995), 58-79.

172 Roy B. Zuck, *Basic Bible Interpretation* (Colorado Springs, CO: David C. Cook Publishing, 1991), 64.

173 Tim LaHaye and Jerry Jenkins, *Are We Living in the Last Days?* (Wheaton, IL: Tyndale House Publishers, 1999), 49-55.

174 John F. Walvoord, *The Blessed Hope and the Tribulation* (Grand Rapids, MI: Zondervan Publishing House, 1976), 87.

175 For extensive historical evidence of this tendency, see Francis X. Gumerlock, *The Day and the Hour* (Atlanta, GA: American Vision, 2000).

176 Russell Chandler, *Doomsday* (Ann Arbor, MI: Servant Publications, 1993), 119.

177 Gleason L. Archer, Jr., "Daniel" in *The Expositor's Bible Commentary*, ed. Frank E. Gaebelein (Grand Rapids, MI: Zondervan Publishing House, 1985), 120.

178 Paul Boyer, *When Time Shall Be No More* (Cambridge, MA: Belknap Press, 1992), 64, 68, 56, 62, 69-70.

179 Ibid., 81-84.

180 Timothy Weber, *Living in the Shadow of the Second Coming* (Chicago: University of Chicago Press, 1987), 182-183; Dwight Wilson, *Armageddon Now!* (Tyler, TX: Institute for Christian Economics, 1991), 114-118, 144-147.

181 C.S. Lewis, "Is Progress Possible?" in *God in the Dock*, ed. Walter Hooper (Grand Rapids, MI: Eerdmans, 1970), 312.

182 Hal Lindsey, *The Late Great Planet Earth* (Grand Rapids, MI: Zondervan Publishing House, 1970), 62.

183 Hal Lindsey, *Planet Earth—2000 A.D.* (Palos Verde, CA: Western Front, Ltd., 1996), 173.

184 Hal Lindsey, *The Late Great Planet Earth* (Grand Rapids, MI: Zondervan Publishing House, 1970), 74; Hal Lindsey, *Planet Earth—2000 A.D.* (Palos Verde, CA: Western Front, Ltd., 1996), 183.

185 Hal Lindsey, *The Late Great Planet Earth* (Grand Rapids, MI: Zondervan Publishing House, 1970), 88-97; Hal Lindsey, *Planet Earth—2000 A.D.* (Palos Verde, CA: Western Front, Ltd., 1996), 225-239.

# Endnotes

[186] Tim LaHaye and Jerry Jenkins, *Are We Living in the Last Days?* (Wheaton, IL: Tyndale House Publishers, 1999), 131-143, 169-172.

[187] Tim LaHaye, *The Beginning of the End* (Wheaton, IL: Tyndale House Publishers, 1972), 165-169. For a side-by-side comparison of the two editions of LaHaye's book, see Richard Abanes, *End-Time Visions* (Nashville, TN: Broadman & Holman Publishers, 1998), 294-296.

[188] Timothy Weber, *Living in the Shadow of the Second Coming* (Chicago: University of Chicago Press, 1987), 201-202.

[189] Paul Boyer, *When Time Shall Be No More* (Cambridge, MA: Belknap Press, 1992), 295-296.

[190] Roger Steer, ed., *The George Müller Treasury* (Westchester, IL: Crossway Books, 1987), 143.

[191] D.A. Carson, *For the Love of God* (Wheaton, IL: Crossway Books, 1998), 1: October 28.

[192] "We are never promised complete understanding of biblical prophecies before their fulfillment. Their main purpose is to keep us expectant, obedient, and trustful and to provide, in their fulfillment, evidence of the faithfulness of God to his word. In the fulfilled events themselves, God will be seen to be true." G.W. Grogan, "Isaiah," in *Expositor's Bible Commentary*, ed. Frank E. Gaebelein (Grand Rapids, MI: Zondervan), 6:15.

[193] R.J. Zwi Werblowsky, "Prophecy, the Land and the People," in Carl F. H. Henry, *Prophecy in the Making*, (Carol Stream, IL: Creation House, 1971), 346.

[194] J. Barton Payne, *Encyclopedia of Biblical Prophecy* (New York: Harper & Row, Publishers, 1973), 674-675.

[195] Even these predictions are not quite as specific as they may at first appear. Jeremiah's prediction of 70 years of exile is best understood as a round number and not a precise length of time. The predictions of Daniel 11:2-39 were fulfilled in identifiable historical events, but the fulfillment of Daniel 11:40-45 is much harder to identify.

[196] Christopher J.H. Wright, *The Message of Ezekiel* (Downers Grove, IL: InterVarsity Press, 2001), 341-342.

[197] Timothy Paul Jones, *Rose Guide to End-Times Prophecy* (Torrance, CA: Rose Publishing, Inc., 2011), 134-136; adapted from G.K. Beale, *The Temple*

*and the Church's Mission* (Downers Grove, IL: InterVarsity Press, 2004), 352-353.

[198] Anthony Hoekema, *The Bible and the Future* (Grand Rapids, MI: Eerdmans, 1979), 142-147.

[199] C.E.B. Cranfield, *The Epistle to the Romans* (Edinburgh: T & T Clark, 1979), 2:576-577; Douglas J. Moo, *The Epistle to the Romans* (Grand Rapids, MI: Eerdmans, 1996), 719-726.

[200] James A. Showers, "Replacement Theology: The Black Sheep of Christendom—Part 1," *Israel My Glory*, March/April 2010, 20.

[201] John Hagee, *In Defense of Israel* (Lake Mary, FL: FrontLine, 2007), 146.

[202] Marvin J. Rosenthal, "For Those Who Can Handle the Truth," *Zion's Fire*, May-June 2013), 3.

[203] Some writers equate Replacement Theology with Covenant or Reformed Theology. See James A. Showers, "The Facts and Flaws of Covenant Theology—Part 1," *Israel My Glory*, September/October 2011, 21-23. But that identification is too broad a generalization. It fails to take into account what Covenant or Reformed Theology emphasizes, and it neglects the variety of beliefs that characterize those Covenant and Reformed theologians.

[204] This summary is based on Michael J. Vlach, "Various Forms of Replacement Theology," *The Masters Seminary Journal* 20 (Spring 2009): 60; James A. Showers, "The Facts and Flaws of Covenant Theology—Part 3," *Israel My Glory*, January/February 2012, 28. See also Tom Ice, "What is Replacement Theology?" accessed January 25, 2012, http://www.pretrib.org/data/pdf/Ice-WhatisReplacementThe.pdf.

[205] Michael J. Vlach, "Various Forms of Replacement Theology," *The Masters Seminary Journal* 20 (Spring 2009): 59-60.

[206] Ibid., 58.

[207] R.T. France, *Jesus and the Old Testament* (Grand Rapids, MI: Baker Book House, 1971), 75-76: John W. Wenham, *Christ and the Bible* (Downers Grove, IL: InterVarsity Press, 1972), 106-108; Tom Wells and Fred Zaspel, *New Covenant Theology* (Frederick, MD: New Covenant Media, 2002), 113; Timothy Paul Jones, *Rose Guide to End-Times Prophecy* (Torrance, CA: Rose Publishing, Inc., 2011), 61-63.

[208] For an excellent short article on Romans 11, see Keith A. Mathison, "The Church and Israel in the New Testament," *Tabletalk*, October 2012, 16-22.

# Endnotes

[209] Ralph Drollinger, "Biblical Speaking, Should America Defend Israel?" *Capitol Ministries Members Bible Study*, July 9, 2012, 3-4.

[210] "So we may sum up. There is a sense (a basic principle or subject matter) in which meaning is stable. There is a fundamental meaning to the text. Such meaning can be clearly stated. What can shift is that to which the meaning applies. Linguistically this shift of meaning is associated with what is called the referent, since a new context often means fresh referents. However, in that later application of meaning, the original meaning is still at work and it is still developing." Darrell Bock, "Single Meaning, Multiple Contexts and Referents," in Kenneth Berding, *Three Views on the New Testament Use of the Old Testament* (Grand Rapids, MI: Zondervan, 2008), 146.

[211] James A. Showers, "The Facts and Flaws of Covenant Theology—Part 3," *Israel My Glory*, January/February 2012, 28.

[212] John Stott, "The Place of Israel," in Stephen Sizer, *Zion's Christian Soldiers?* (Downers Grove, IL: InterVarsity Press, 2007), 169-170.

[213] C.E.B. Cranfield, *The Epistle to the Romans* (Edinburgh: T & T Clark, 1979), 2:572-588; Douglas J. Moo, *The Epistle to the Romans* (Grand Rapids, MI: Eerdmans, 1996), 710-739; David E. Holwerda, *Jesus & Israel* (Grand Rapids, MI: Eerdmans, 1995), 147-176.

[214] Craig Blaising, "The Future of Israel as a Theological Question," *Journal of the Evangelical Theological Society* 44, no. 3 (2001): 437. Dunn characterizes it as a "strong consensus." James D.G. Dunn, *Romans 9-16* (Dallas, TX: Word Publishing, 1988), 681.

[215] David Brog, *Standing with Israel* (Lake Mary, FL: FrontLine, 2006), 14.

[216] James A. Showers, "Replacement Theology: The Black Sheep of Christendom—Part 1," *Israel My Glory*, March/April 2010, 20.

[217] James A. Showers, "Replacement Theology: The Black Sheep of Christendom—Part 4," *Israel My Glory*, September/October 2010, 33.

[218] Clarence H. Wagner, Jr., "The Error of Replacement Theology," *Bridges for Peace*, May 9, 2002.

[219] Tom Ice, "What is Replacement Theology?" accessed January 25, 2012, http://www.pre-trib.org/data/pdf/Ice-WhatisReplacementThe.pdf.

[220] Quoted in Colin Chapman, *Whose Promised Land?* (Grand Rapids, MI: Baker Book House, 2002), 46.

[221] Rosemary Ruether, *Faith and Fratricide* (Eugene, OR: Wipf and Stock

Publishers, 1995), 180, quoted in David Brog, *Standing with Israel* (Lake Mary, FL: FrontLine, 2006), 25.

[222] Raul Hilberg, *The Destruction of the European Jews* (Chicago: Quadrangle Books, 1961), 5-6.

[223] Quoted in David Brog, *Standing with Israel* (Lake Mary, FL: FrontLine, 2006), 28-29.

[224] Stott, "The Place of Israel," in Stephen Sizer, *Zion's Christian Soldiers?* (Downers Grove, IL: InterVarsity Press, 2007), 169-170.

[225] Timothy P. Weber, *On the Road to Armageddon* (Grand Rapids, MI: Baker Book House, 2004), 231-234.

[226] Gershom Gorenberg, *The End of Days* (New York: The Free Press, 2000), 226.

[227] Ami Kaufman, "MK Michael Ben-Ari Rips Up New Testament, Throws It in Trash," *+972 Magazine*, July 17, 2012, accessed September 3, 2012, http://972mag.com/mk-michael-ben-ari-tears-up-new-testament-throws-it-in-trash/51196/.

[228] David Brog, *Standing with Israel* (Lake Mary, FL: FrontLine, 2006), 204.

[229] Vlach distinguishes between a "strong" and "moderate" form of theological supersessionism. "Strong" supersessionism asserts that Israel will not experience a large-scale or national conversion while "moderate" supersessionism holds that the nation of Israel will experience a mass turning to Christ. Michael J. Vlach, "Various Forms of Replacement Theology," *The Masters Seminary Journal* 20 (Spring 2009): 65-69. Vlach bases his analysis on Richard Kendell Soulen, *The God of Israel and Christian Theology* (Minneapolis: Fortress, 1996), 30-34.

[230] Brog David Brog, *Standing with Israel* (Lake Mary, FL: FrontLine, 2006), 261, n. 39.

[231] Other critics of Replacement Theology do admit that it does not necessarily lead to anti-Semitism, but their writings still leave the strong impression that it is the likely outcome. See Gary G. Cohen, "Is God Done with Israel?" *Zion's Fire*, July-August 2010, 20; James A. Showers, "The New Anti-Semitism," *Israel My Glory*, January/February 2013, 15.

[232] "Full transcript of Netanyahu speech at UN General Assembly," *Haaretz*, September 24, 2011, accessed August 7, 2013, http://www.haaretz.com/

news/diplomacy-defense/full-transcript-of-netanyahu-speech-at-un-general-assembly-1.386464.

[233] Global Firepower, April 1, 2015, accessed August 13, 2015, http://www.globalfirepower.com.

[234] Institute for Middle East Understanding. "What is the Military Capability of Israel?" November 25, 2005, accessed January 19, 2015, http://imeu.org/article/what-is-the-military-capability-of-israel.

[235] Avraham Burg, *The Holocaust is Over: We Must Rise from Its Ashes* (New York: Palgrave Macmillan, 2008), 40, 209.

[236] Shlomo Ben-Ami, *Scars of War, Wounds of Peace* (New York: Oxford University Press, 2006), xii, 72, 312.

[237] Brookings Institution, "Letter from President Ford to Prime Minister Rabin September 1, 1975," accessed July 23, 2013, http://www.brookings.edu/~/media/Press/Books/2005/peaceprocess3/Appendix%20C.pdf.

[238] Joe Biden quoted in "US Support for Israel Must Continue Forever," *Jerusalem Post*, November 8, 2010, accessed July 26, 2013, http://www.jpost.com/International/US-support-for-Israel-must-continue-forever-says-Biden.

[239] John J. Mearsheimer and Stephen M. Walt, *The Israel Lobby and U.S. Foreign Policy* (New York: Farrar, Straus and Giroux, 2007), 27-28.

[240] Congressional Research Service. *U.S. Foreign Aid to Israel*, by Jeremy M. Sharp, Summary. June 10, 2015, accessed August 13, 2015, http://www.fas.org/sgp/crs/mideast/RL33222.pdf.

[241] Congressional Research Service. *U.S. Foreign Aid to the Palestinians*, by Jim Zanotti, Summary, 11, 15. July 3, 2014, accessed January 23, 2015, http://www.fas.org/sgp/crs/mideast/RS22967.pdf.

[242] Allyn Fisher-Ilan, "U.S. Senator Threatens Aid Cut to Palestinians over ICC Move," Reuters, January 19, 2015, accessed January 20, 2015, http://uk.reuters.com/article/2015/01/19/uk-usa-israel-palestinians-idUKKBN0KS24V20150119.

[243] Congressional Research Service. *Israel: Background and U.S. Relations*, by Jim Zanotti, 48. June 1, 2015, accessed August 13, 2015, https://www.fas.org/sgp/crs/mideast/RL33476.pdf.

[244] David Ignatius, "Why the Mideast Peace Process is in Tatters," *Washington Post*, May 16, 2014, accessed May 16, 2014, http://www.washingtonpost.com/opinions/david-ignatius-why-the-mideast-peace-process-is-in-

tatters/2014/05/15/c8345e78-dc5b-11e3-8009-71de85b9c527_story.html.

[245] Celine Hagbard, "U.S. House Unanimously Passes Resolution Supporting Israeli Attack on Gaza," July 15, 2014, accessed January 21, 2015, http://www.imemc.org/article/68479; Chris Carlson, "U.S. Senate Unanimously Passes Resolution Supporting Israeli Assault on Gaza," July 18, 2014, accessed January 21, 2015, http://www.imemc.org /article/68523.

[246] "Christian Leaders Call for End to Unconditional US Military Aid." *Kairos USA*, accessed August 7, 2013, http://www.kairosusa.org/?q=node/55.

[247] "Enough is Enough," Jewish Council for Public Affairs. October 17, 2012, accessed August 7, 2013, http://engage.jewishpublicaffairs.org/blog/comments.jsp?blog_ entry_KEY=6599.

[248] B'Tselem, "About B'Tselem," accessed August 7, 2013, http://www.btselem.org/about_btselem.

[249] "The Combatant Letter," *Courage to Refuse,* accessed August 7, 2013, http://www.seruv.org.il/defaulteng.asp.

[250] "The Pilot's Letter," *Courage to Refuse,* accessed August 7, 2013, http://www.seruv.org.il/english/article .asp?msgid=55&type=news.

[251] "The Commandos Letter," *Courage to Refuse,* accessed August 7, 2013, http://www.seruv.org.il/english /news_item.asp?msgid=85.

[252] "The Olga Document," *Not in My Name,* accessed January 21, 2015, http://www.nimn.org/Perspectives /israeli_voices/000233.php.

[253] Breaking the Silence, "About Us," accessed August 7, 2013, http://www.breakingthesilence.org.il/about /organization.

[254] Avi Shlaim, *The Iron Wall* 2nd ed. (New York: W.W. Norton & Company, 2014), 813.

[255] Ahron Bergman, *Cursed Victory* (New York: Pegasus Books, 2014), 307-308.

[256] Quoted in Rula Jebreal, "Moshe Dayan's Widow Ruth: Zionist Dream Has Run Its Course," *The Daily Beast,* October 30, 2011, accessed July 12, 2013, http://www.thedailybeast.com/newsweek/2011/10/30/moshe-dayans-widow-ruth-zionist-dream-has-run-its-course.html.

[257] Ari Shavit, *My Promised Land* (New York: Spiegel & Grau, 2013), 402.

[258] Avraham Burg, *The Holocaust is Over: We Must Rise from Its Ashes* (New York: Palgrave Macmillan, 2008), 87.

[259] "Endorse the J Street Ad. Obama and Netanyahu: Act Now to Achieve

## Endnotes

a Two-state Peace," *Daily Kos*, May 19, 2011, accessed July 11, 2013, http://www.dailykos.com/story/2011/05/19/977507/-Endorse-the-J-Street-Ad-Obama-and-Netanyahu-Act-now-to-achieve-a-two-state-peace#.

[260] Rabbi Michael Lerner, *Embracing Israel / Palestine* (Berkeley, CA: North Atlantic Books, 2012), 65.

[261] Brant Rosen, *Wrestling in the Daylight* (Charlottesville, VA: Just World Books, 2012), 20.

[262] John B. Judis, *Genesis: Truman, American Jews, and the Origins of the Arab/Israeli Conflict* (New York: Farrar, Straus and Giroux, 2014), 350-353.

[263] Christians United for Israel, "The Israel Pledge," 2010 November, accessed August 7, 2013, http://www.cufi.org/site/PageServer.

[264] John S. Feinberg, "Dispensationalism and Support for the State of Israel," (lecture, Christ at the Checkpoint Conference, March 17, 2010, accessed August 7, 2013, http://www.christatthecheckpoint.com/lectures /John%20Feinberg.pdf.

[265] Wayne Grudem, *Politics According to the Bible* (Grand Rapids, MI: Zondervan, 2010), 470.

[266] A surprising exception to this tendency comes from David Larsen. "My concern is that Christians out of loyal identification with the fortunes of the Jewish state (which I profoundly share) cease to be concerned about justice for all. Read the almost daily accounts—the mounting tensions in Jerusalem, the strife between old Arab and Jewish families, and the struggles of any Palestinian family in Israel—*and weep*. We do not honor our God by deprecating and despising any people—Jew or Arab. To treat others justly; that is our calling." Unfortunately, Larsen wrote his book in 1995, and his concern is not repeated by contemporary Christian Zionists. David L. Larsen, *Jews, Gentiles, and the Church* (Grand Rapids, MI: Discovery House, 1995), 329.

[267] Wayne Grudem, *Politics According to the Bible* (Grand Rapids, MI: Zondervan, 2010), 461.

[268] Gary Burge, *Jesus and the Land* (Grand Rapids, MI: Baker Publishing Group, 2010), 123.

[269] Stephen Sizer, *Christian Zionism* (Downers Grove, IL: InterVarsity Press, 2004), 93.

[270] O.T. Allis, "Israel's Transgression in Palestine," *Christianity Today*, December 24, 1956, 9.

[271] Elisabeth Elliot, *Furnace of the Lord* (Garden City, New York: Doubleday & Company, 1969), 123-124.

[272] Colin Chapman, *Whose Promised Land?* (Grand Rapids, MI: Baker Book House, 2002), 10.

[273] "An Open Letter to Evangelicals and Other Interested Parties: The People of God, the Land of Israel, and the Impartiality of the Gospel," accessed August 7, 2013, http://www.pcabakersfield.com/articles /open_letter_to_evangelicals.pdf.

[274] "A Moment of Truth: A Word of Faith, Hope, and Love from the Heart of Palestinian Suffering," *Kairos Palestine 2009*, accessed August 7, 2013, http://www.kairospalestine.ps/sites/default/Documents/English.pdf. See also "Call to Action: U.S. Response to the Kairos Palestine Document," accessed August 7, 2013, http://www.kairosusa .org/images/kairosusabooklet.pdf.

[275] David P. Gushee and Glen H. Stassen, "An Open Letter to America's Christian Zionists," *The New Evangelical Partnership for the Common Good*. September 19, 2011, accessed August 17, 2013, http://www .newevangelicalpartnership.org/?q=node/139.